Annals of the Polish Rom. Cath. Union
Archives and Museum

VOL. V. 1940

POLISH PIONEERS
OF CALIFORNIA

by

MIECISLAUS HAIMAN

POLISH R. C. UNION OF AMERICA
CHICAGO. ILL.. 1940.

Published by:

R & E RESEARCH ASSOCIATES
18581 McFarland Ave., Saratoga, California
4843 Mission St., San Francisco, California

REPRINT San Francisco, 1969

EDITOR   PUBLISHER
ADAM S. ETEROVICH   ROBERT D. REED

Library of Congress Catalog Card Number
73-86457

579

The P. R. C. U. Archives and Museum

The P. R. C. U. Archives and Museum made new and remarkable progress in the year of 1939-40. It acquired additional spacious quarters; all its collections continued to grow quickly; the attendance was larger than in former years. However, the sad conditions of the world were not without their influence on our institution. Not only were all connections with Poland and some other countries cut off but the devastations of war and the total destruction and plunder of all Polish museums and libraries by the invader destroyed the hope of ever rehabilitating all the Polish Americana which the P. R. C. U. Archives and Museum started to collect abroad, thanks to the wholehearted cooperation and generosity of Polish and other institutions.

The dedication of the enlarged quarters of the P. R. C. U. Archives and Museum took place on October 8, 1939. It was preceded by Mass at St. Joseph's R. C. Church. President Joseph L. Kania of the Polish Roman Catholic Union presided over an appropriate program at the premises. The new quarters were dedicated by the Very Rev. Canon Casimir Gronkowski, Chaplain of the Polish Roman Catholic Union, assisted by the Rev. Paul Janeczko of Spring Valley, Ill., Vice-Chaplain, and by the Rev. Peter H. Pyterek. Hon. Wladyslaw Wankowicz, Counsellor of the Polish Embassy in Washington, D. C., unveiled the monument containing soil from historical Polish battlefields, donated by the Światowy Związek Polaków z Zagranicy (the World Alliance of Poles Abroad) of Warsaw and shipped to America just before the war.

Mrs. Honorata B. Wołowska, President of the Polish Women's Alliance, officially presented the

Museum with the monumental painting "Pulaski at Savannah", gift of the 18th Convention of her organization. Addresses were made by the Hon. Counsellor Wankowicz, Very Rev. Canon Gronkowski, Mrs. Wolowska, Mr. Peter Kozlowski, Vice-President of the Polish National Alliance, and Hon. Walter Orlikowski. Many congratulatory messages were read, among others from His Exc. Ignace Jan Paderewski.

On October 7, 1939, the Polish Society of History and Museum of America held its Second Convention in the Museum, presided over by the Very Rev. Gronkowski, Chairman of the Museum Committee. Addresses were made by the Hon. Dr. Waclaw Gawronski, Consul General of Poland at Chicago, and President Kania. Alphonse S. Wolanin, Ph. D., Archivist of the Museum, read a paper on the methods of collecting of historical material. The report of the Custodian was accepted.

The Convention elected Mrs. Honorata B. Wolowska and Theophilus Starzynski, M. D., of Pittsburgh, Pa., President of the Polish Falcons of America, new members of the Museum Committee to fill the vacancy of the late Prof. Joseph Birkenmajer, Ph. D.

Following are some statistics from the report of the Custodian for the year 1939:

The Museum was visited by 8,096 persons during that year, which number comprised 86 group-visits, 62 of which were composed of school children. Twenty one groups were composed of people of other national origin than Polish. Ninety one students used the material at the premises and 65 institutions and persons received answers by mail on questions mostly pertaining to the history of Poles in this country, or of Poland. One hundred eighty five objects were donated to or exchanged with 15 institutions and persons, and 37 objects were loaned to 14 reliable institutions and persons.

The Museum arranged several temporary exhibits on timely subjects during the last year.

6

The Museum extends its most sincere thanks to all those who by their financial support or by donations of objects helped to make it a more useful institution.

The P. R. C. U. Archives and Museum endeavors to be of the greatest possible service to all seeking any information on the history of the Poles in America. We invite all such students to make free use of these facilities, and the Custodian will gladly make convenient arrangements.

The Archives and Museum is open to the public on Tuesdays from 1 to 4:30 P. M., on Fridays from 7 to 8:30 P. M. and Saturdays from 10 to 12 A. M. Schools and societies may visit in groups at any time, upon previously notifying the Custodian. Admission is free, no entrance fee being charged.

The P. R. C. U. Archives and Museum collects anything which has any bearing on the history of the Poles in the United States. It will appreciate the donation of any of the following:

Books and pamphlets on the history and biography of the Poles in the United States; reports of Polish-American Societies and Institutions of any kind; books and pamphlets by American-Poles on any subject; books on Poland or any Polish subject in any language, published in the United States; files of Polish-American newspapers or magazines, complete volumes or single numbers; portraits of Polish-American pioneers and eminent persons; photographs and pictures illustrating Polish life in America; autographs and manuscripts, maps, medals, badges, uniforms and banners of Polish-American Societies, etc.

Communications and gifts may be addressed to the Custodian of the P. R. C. U. Archives and Museum, M. Haiman, 984-986 Milwaukee Ave., Chicago, Ill.

Prof. Joseph Birkenmajer

Prof. Joseph Birkenmajer, Ph. D., was born in Czernichow, Poland, on March 19, 1897, as a member of a family well known in the annals of Polish science for several generations. His father, Ludwik A. Birkenmajer, was a famous professor of mathematics at the Jagiellonian University of Cracow.

Prof. Joseph Birkenmajer took part in the first World War as soldier of the Polish Legions and spent several years as prisoner of war in Siberia. After many perilous adventures he managed to escape to Poland and fought in the Polish-Bolshevik War of 1920.

Immediately thereafter he resumed his studies and received a Ph. D., degree from the University of Warsaw. He early became nationally known as a philologist and writer. He published many translations and many volumes of original writings ranging from studies on old Greek writers to graceful novels and poems. In 1937 he came to the United States as professor of Polish philology at the University of Wisconsin. Returning to Poland in 1939, he was killed on September 26, 1939 in the defense of Warsaw.

For two years he was a member of the Museum Committee and our institution is much indebted to him for his untiring efforts to serve it on all occasions.

R. I. P.

List of Members of the Polish Society of History and Museum of America

(From July 1, 1939, to July 1, 1940)

(There are three classes of membership; regular with a fee of $1.00 yearly, supporting with a fee of $5.00 yearly and perpetual with a single fee of $100.00. The numbers beside names are registration numbers and signify the order in which members joined the Society).

PERPETUAL MEMBERS

JOSEPH J. BARĆ, Chicago, Ill.

JOSEPH C. NIEC, LL. D., Chicago, Ill.

STANLEY T. KUSPER, Ph. B., LL. B., Chicago, Ill.

STANISLAUS C. LEŚNIAK, Chicago, Ill.

UNITED LOCAL COUNCILS OF THE POLISH ROMAN CATHOLIC UNION OF AMERICA, Chicago, Ill.

WALTER STANCZEWSKI, Chicago, Ill.

FRANK A. BRANDT, Chicago, Ill.

WALLACE S. KULPA, Chicago, Ill.

WOMEN'S DEPARTMENT OF THE POLISH ROMAN CATHOLIC UNION OF AMERICA, Chicago, Ill.

JOSEPH L. KANIA, Chicago, Ill.

FRANCIS BIELAWA, Chicago, Ill.

ALBERT MENKICKI, Chicago, Ill.

ST. CECILIA'S SOCIETY, No. 14, Polish Roman Catholic Union, Chicago, Ill.

THE MOCZYDLOWSKI FAMILY AND "PRZEWODNIK POLSKI", St. Louis, Mo.

FILIP W. TOMASZEWSKI, Chicago, Ill.

JOSEPH KOWIESKI, Chicago, Ill.

MICHAEL DYDYMUS, Chicago, Ill.

CASIMIR S. WICZAS, Chicago, Ill.

ANTHONY A. ZUWALSKI, Chicago, Ill.

LADISLAUS C. MADAY, Chicago, Ill.

FRANCIS A. DANIEL, Cicero, Ill.

JOHN ZIELINSKI, Holyoke, Mass.

MRS. ANTOINETTE WŁODARSKA-CZERNIAK, Chicago, Ill.

POLISH-AMERICAN GOLD STAR FATHERS' AND MOTHERS' ASSOCIATION, Chicago, Ill.

ST. ALOYSIUS SOCIETY, No. 375, Polish Roman Catholic Union, Chicago, Ill.

ALFRED J. KOLOMYSKI, Chicago, Ill.

CHARLES J. KALETA, Chicago, Ill.

JOHN W. WOZNY, Chicago, Ill.

THE LATE JOHN AND CONSTANCE CZEKAŁA, Chicago, Ill.

DR. LADISLAUS A. DZIUK, Chicago, Ill.

REV. LOUIS A. STACHOWICZ, Philadelphia, Pa

REV. JOHN LANGOW, South Deerfield, Mass.

SOCIETY OF OUR LADY OF GIDLE, No. 498, Polish Roman Catholic Union, Chicago, Ill.

DR. CHARLES H. WACHTL, Philadelphia, Pa.

REV. FELICJAN SISTERS, O. S. F.

SUPPORTING MEMBERS

1. Dr. Bronislaus L. Smykowski, Bridgeport, Conn.
4. Dr. Romuald O. Ostrowski, Hammond, Ind.
7. Francis S. Barć, Chicago, Ill.
8. Julian Groszewski, Chicago, Ill.
9. Casimir J. B. Wronski, Chicago, Ill.
14. Rev. Anthony Wojcieszczuk, Suffield, Conn.
28. Joseph Walaszek, Chicago, Ill.
29. Andrew Kazmierczak, Chicago, Ill.
63. Clarence N. Affolter, Chicago, Ill.
74. Rev. Paul Janeczko, Spring Valley, Ill.
112. Joseph Sroka, Chicago, Ill.
132. Circuit 47, Polish R. C. Union, Chicago, Ill.
155. Dr. Francis J. Tenczar, Chicago, Ill.
166. Circuit 72, Polish R. C Union, Worcester, Mass.
186. Rev. Francis X. Guzy, Buffalo, N. Y.
187. Rev. Peter Klekotka, Chester, Pa.
191. Rev. Bernard K. Szudziński, Cicero, Ill.
198. Francis J. Tomczak, Chicago, Ill.
251. Rev. Joseph Maj, Jersey City, N. J.
253. Rev. Ladislaus Sikora, Hyde Park, Mass.
260. Dr. Joseph Kij, Lackawanna, N. Y.
263. Rev. Francis J. Kachnowski, Posen, Illl.
264. Very Rev. Lawrence Cyman, O. M. C., Chicopee, Mass.
268. Lawrence Zygmunt, Chicago, Ill.
280. The late Prof. Dr. Joseph Birkenmajer, Warsaw, Poland.
284. Rev. Boleslaus Milinkiewicz, Detroit, Mich.
331. Rt. Rev. Msgr. Dr. Alexander A. Pitass, Buffalo, N. Y.
333. John J. Olejniczak, Chicago, Ill.
343. Dr. Marian Kostrubala, Chicago, Ill.
352. St. James the Apostle School, Chicago, Ill.
353. The Rev. Bernardine Sisters, Reading, Pa
356. I. Dovia, Chicago, Ill.
394. St. James' Society, No. 795, Polish R. C. Union, Chicago, Ill.
405. The Polish Messenger of the Sacred Heart, Inc., Chicago, Ill.
418. St. Hyacinth's Society, No. 19, Polish R. C. Union, Chicago, Ill
421. Vincent Cygan, Chicago, Ill.
422. Ignatius Laszkiewicz, Chicago, Ill.
480. Stanislaus P. Turkiewicz, Buffalo, N. Y.
489. Rev. Paul W. Piechocki, Middletown, Conn.
490. Rev. Sebastian Jerzak, Conshohocken, Pa.
494. Stanislaus A. Błonski, San Francisco, Calif.
519. Rev. Stephen Krol, Erie, Pa.
521. Hon. John Lesinski, M. C., Dearborn, Mich.
525. St. Adalbert's School, Chicago, Ill.
536. Circuit 5, Polish R. C. Union, Pittsburgh, Pa.
546. St. Stanislaus' Kostka Society, No. 421, Polish R. C. Union, Holyoke, Mass.
573. Very Rev. Mother Provincial M. Hilaria, Sisters of the Holy Family of Nazareth, Pitttsburgh, Pa.
574. Hon. Leonard W. Schuetz, M. C., Chicago, Ill.
582. Hon. Paul Drymalski, Chicago, Ill.
588. Mrs. Constance and Mr. Francis Chamski, Detroit, Mich.
593. Mrs. Caroline Rzeznik, St. Louis, Mo.
599. Dr. Roman Sadowski, Detroit, Mich.
601. Holy Trinity School, Chicago, Ill.
602. St. Stanislaus, B. & M., School, Chicago, Ill.
608. Polish Dentists' Association, Chicago, Ill.
609. Lourdes High School, Chicago, Ill.
612. The late Joseph Barc, Jackson, Mich.
621. Queen of the Polish Crown Society, No. 317, Polish R. C. Union, Chicago, Ill.
622. Leo C. Nyka, Chicago, Ill.
625. St Hedwig's Society, No. 24, Polish R. C. Union, Michigan City, Ind.
632. Rev. Peter P. Walkowiak, Hamtramck, Mich.

10

634. St. Vincent a Paulo Society, No. 463, Polish R. C. Union, East Haven, Conn.
644. Prof. Eric P. Kelly, Dartmouth College, Hanover, N. H.
647. Brigadier General Joseph E. Barzynski, U. S. A., Washington, D. C.
654. Major Benjamin T. Anuskewicz, U. S. A. R., Brooklyn, N. Y.
658. Harry Rażewski, Schenectady, N. Y.
674. Rt. Rev. Msgr. Ignatius Szudrowicz, Jersey City, N. J.
676. Very Rev. Justine Figas, O. M. C., Buffalo, N. Y.

5. Anthony Brzenk, Chicago, Ill.
10. Anthony Kozubal, Chicago, Ill.
11. Miecislaus Haiman, Chicago, Ill.
12. Rev. Apolonius Tyszka, Pittsburgh, Pa.
13. Rev. John P. Skowronski, Easthampton, Mass.
16. Mrs. Theophila Sawicka, Detroit, Mich.
22. Mrs. Anna Kusza, Suffield, Conn.
25. Mrs. Rosalie Slosarz, La Porte, Ind.
33. John A. Troike, Chicago, Ill.
36. Very Rev. Msgr. Alexander Syski, Orchard Lake, Mich.
38. Bronislaus Lendo, Detroit, Mich.
42. St. Casimir's Society, No. 389. Polish R. C. Union. Meriden, Conn.
44. St. Hedwig's Society, No. 1005, Polish R. C. Union, Kenosha, Wis.
45. Circuit 129, Polish R. C. Union, Cicero, Ill.
46. Society of King Casimir, No. 126, Polish R. C. Union, Chicago, Ill.
47. Gen. Haller Society, No. 625, Polish R. C. Union, Chicago, Ill.
48. Mrs. Antoinette Druciak, New Bedford, Mass.
53. Francis Głowacki, Chicago, Ill.
58. Anthony Patraszewski, Chicago, Ill.
60. Max A. Lipiński, Chicago, Ill.
64. Miss Flavia Wiedemann, Chicago, Ill.
67. John Marmurowicz, Milwaukee, Wis.
69. Casimir Rechcygiel, Chicago, Ill.
73. Stanislaus Faderski, Pittston, Pa.
81. St. Bronislava's Polish Women Society, No. 388, Polish R. C. Union, South Chicago, Ill.
84. Stephen Grabowski, Pittsburgh, Pa.
85. Society of Polish Knights, No. 911, Polish R. C. Union, Bentleyville, Pa.
86. St. Stanislaus' Society, No. 57, Polish R C. Union, San Francisco, Calif.
90. Arthur L. Waldo, New York, N. Y.
91. Miss Sabina Logisz, Chicago, Ill.
92. Miss Loretta Burda, Argo, Ill.
99. St. Mary's Society, No. 63, Polish R. C. Union, La Salle, Ill.
100. St. Stanislaus Kostka Society, No. 1009, Polish R. C. Union, Fall River, Mass.
104. St. Joseph's Society, No. 141, Polish R. C. Union, Cheboygan, Mich.
105. Polish Women's Society of Our Lady of Perpetual Help, No. 40, Polish R. C. Union, Chicago, Ill.
107. Immaculate Conception of the B. V. M. Society, No. 581, Polish R. C. Union, Southington, Conn.
110. Society of St. Therese of the Child Jesus, No. 1245, Polish R. C. Union, Middletown, Conn.
113. Roman Kopec, Chicago, Ill.
115. Society of St. Rose of Lima, No. 272, Polish R. C. Union. Chicago, Ill.
116. Dr. Edward Nowicki, Gary, Ind.
118. St. Cecilia's Society, No. 943, Polish R. C. Union, Chicago, Ill
119. Ignatius K. Werwiński, South Bend, Ind.
121. Society of the Sacred Heart of Jesus, No. 306, Polish R. C Union, Chicago, Ill.
121. Society of the Sacred Heart of Jesus, No. 308, Polish R. C Union, Chicago, Ill.
127. Circuit 50, Polish R. C. Union, Posen, Ill.
129. Circuit 53, Polish R. C. Union, Gary, Ind.
131. St. Anthony's Society, No. 330, Polish R. C. Union, Chicago, Ill
134. Circuit 12, Polish R. C .Union, Shamokin, Pa.
135. Society of St. Therese of the Child Jesus, No. 1147, Polish R. C. Union, Chicago, Ill.

139. Society of the Good Shepherd, No. 494, Polish R. C. Union, Chicago, Ill.
141. St. Joseph's Society, No. 460, Polish R. C. Union, Taylor, Pa.
144. Circuit 19, Polish R. C. Union, Chicago, Ill.
145. Circuit 18, Polish R. C. Union, Chicago, Ill.
146. Circuit 8, Polish R. C. Union, Detroit, Mich.
147. St. Stanislaus' B. M. Society, No. 1032, Polish R. C. Union, Posen, Ill.
148. Society of Knights of St. Stanislaus B. M., No. 327, Polish R. C. Union, Uniontown, Pa.
149. St. John the Baptist Society, No. 1076, Polish R. C. Union, Knowlton, Wis.
151. Bill Furmanski, Chicago, Ill.
157. Mrs. Anna Berlacin, Gardner, Mass.
160. Our Lady of the Polish Crown Society, No. 413, Polish R. C. Union, East Chicago, Ind.
161. St. Lucian's Society, No. 286, Polish R. C. Union, New Britain, Conn.
170. St. Joseph's Society, No. 515, Pol. R. C. Union, Herkimer, N. Y.
172. Gen. Casimir Pulaski's Society, No. 1329, Polish R. C. Union Chicago, Ill.
173. Francis Łukaszewicz, Buffalo, N. Y.
174. St. Stanislaus B. M. Society, No. 833, Polish R. C. Union, Norwich, Conn.
175. St. Florian's Society, No. 408, Polish R. C. Union, Chicago, Ill.
176. Rev. Joseph Piszczałka, Nashua, N. H.
177. St. Joseph's Society, No. 1268, Polish R. C. Union, Nashua, N. H.
179. Sacred Heart of Jesus Society, No. 471, Polish R. C. Union, Chicago, Ill.
180. Mrs. Eve Biczek, Chicago, Ill.
181. Mrs. Anna Kosieracka, Chicago, Ill.
182. Mrs. Pelagia Zdanowska, Chicago, Ill.
183. Mrs. Josephine Gorska, Chicago, Ill.
188. Rev. Francis Kowalski, Ennis, Texas.
189. St. Hedwig's Polish Women Society, No. 905, Polish R. C Union, Hamtramck, Mich.
190. Stanislaus Butynski, Hammond, Ind.
192. Felix Pawlowski, New Kensington, Pa.
193. St. Joseph's Society, No. 314, Polish R. C. Union, North Chicago, Ill.
194. Society of Polish Women of the Heart of Mary, No. 804, Polish R. C. Union, North Chicago, Ill.
195. Circuit 121, Polish R. C. Union, North Chicago, Ill.
199. Circuit 103, Polish R. C. Union, Philadelphia, Pa.
200. John S. Konopa, Chicago, Ill.
201. Society of Polish Women in Chicago, No. 1198, Polish R. C Union, Chicago, Ill.
206. Joseph S. Kaszubowski, Buffalo, N. Y.
208. Catholic Youth Club, Chicago, Ill.
210. Stanislaus Ciborowski, St. Louis, Mo.
212. Circuit 71, Polish R. C. Union, South River, N. J.
214. James Firszt, Chicago, Ill.
216. St. Adalbert's B. M. Society, No. 204, Polish R. C. Union, Whiting, Ind.
220. Society of the Polish Crown, No. 296, Polish R. C. Union, Chicago, Ill
227. Miss Mary Lew, Chicago, Ill.
230. Mrs. Monica Krawczyk, Minneapolis, Minn.
237. Joseph and Mary Rowinski, Plainville, Conn.
238. Ladisiaus Janeczek, Passaic, N. J.
241. Circuit No. 42, Polish R. C. Union, Chicago, Ill.
246. August Niemczyk, St. Louis, Mo.
256. Rev. Bronislaus Socha, Bloomfield, N. J.
257. Rev. Stanislaus Sierakowski, Buffalo, N. Y.
266. Rev. Theodore Rekosiak, Avon, Minn.
269. Miss Florence Turowski, Youngstown, O.
270. Mr. and Mrs. Joseph Leffner, Chicago, Ill.

278. The Pulaski Society, Brooklyn, N. Y.
286. Very Rev. Dr. Ladislaus Krzyzosiak, Orchard, Lake, Mich.
287. Rev. Anthony Maksymik, Orchard Lake, Mich.
301. Mary Kozłowska, Hamtramck, Mich.
504. Rev. Edward Skrocki, Orchard Lake, Mich.
307. Circuit 62, Polish R. C. Union, Taylor, Pa.
308. Anthony Tracz, New Bedford, Mass.
315. Mrs. Theresa Lewandowska, Chicago, Ill.
316. Holy Innocents School, Chicago, Ill.
317. St. Hedwig's Polish Women Society, No. 357, Polish R. C. Union, Chicago, Ill.
320. Bronislaus S. Kamienski, Pittsburgh, Pa.
321. Mrs. Frances Falkowska, Chicago, Ill.
326. Miss Sophie Ziołkowska, Chicago, Ill.
328. Isadore Skrobilowski, Brooklyn, N. Y.
329 Anthony Skiba, Brooklyn, N. Y.
330. A. Nosek, Brooklyn, N. Y.
332. John Niklibore, Chicago, Ill.
339. Mrs. Harriet L. Turalski, Chicago, Ill.
341. Miss Stephanie L. Kolos, Pittsburgh, Pa.
342. Miss Agnes Kaźmierczak, Chicago, Ill.
346. Stanislaus Jankowski, Jr., Chicago, Ill.
346. Circuit Nr. 14, Polish R. C. Union, Chicago, Ill.
348. Mr. and Mrs. S. Poskoczim, Chicago, Ill.
354. John Perowicz, St. Louis, M.
362. Joseph T. Marzec, Chicago, Ill.
363. Valentine Skoczylas, Chicago, Ill.
365. Miss Mary Skoczylas, Chicago, Ill.
372. John Uczciwek, Chicago, Ill.
374. Mr. and Mrs. John Olejniczak, Jr., Chicago, Ill.
375. Miss Estelle Osucha, Chicago, Ill.
378. Mrs. Harriet Tobiasiewicz, Chicago, Ill.
381. J hn Danek, Chicago, Ill.
383. Alexander Loboda, Chicago, Ill.
384. St. Andrew's Society, No. 233, Polish R. C. Union, Chicago, Ill.
386. Anthony Szott, Turners Falls, Mass.
388. St. Joseph's Society, No. 290, Polish R. C. Union, Chicago, Ill
389. St. Barbara's Society, No. 521, Polish R. C. Union, Chicago, Ill.
390. Joseph Moskal, Chicago, Ill.
391. St. Joseph's Society, No. 567, Polish R. C. Union, Argo, Ill
393. Society of Polish Women of St. Apolonia, No. 482, Polish R. C. Union, Chicago, Ill.
395. Society of the Heart of Mary, No. 683, Polish R. C. Union, Chicago Ill.
397. St. Hedwig's Society, No. 1115, Polish R. C. Union, Albany, New York.
399. Society of Our Lady of Perpetual Help, No. 262, Polish R. C. Union, Hartford, Conn.
404. Society of St. Andrew the Apostle, No. 143, Polish R. C. Union, Calumet City, Ill.
406. Society of the Sacred Heart of Jesus, No. 1345, Polish R. C. Union, River Rouge, Mich.
408. St. Joseph's Society, No. 213, Polish R. C. Union, Wheeling, W. Va.
409. Joseph Wróbel, Chicago, Ill.
410. Joseph Przebieglec, Newark, N. J.
412. Society of our Lady of Czestochowa, No. 36, Polish R. C. Union, Lorain, O.
415. King John III Sobieski Society, No. 16, Polish R. C. Union, Chicago, Ill.
419. Miss Angela Mikulowna, Chicago, Ill.
420. St. Adalbert's Society, No. 258, Polish R. C. Union, Gary, Ind.
430. St. Barbara's Polish Women Society, No. 354, Polish R. C. Union, South Chicago, Ill.
432. St. Agnes' Society, No. 623, Polish R. C. Union, New Britain, Conn.
433. Miss Julia Musial, Chicago, Ill.
437. Society of Polish Women under the patronage of Our Lady of

14

Good Counsel, No. 73, Polish R. C. Union, Chicago, Ill.
441. Mrs. Stephanie Eminowicz-Waldo, New York, N. Y.
443. Society of Our Lady of Tuchow, No. 443, Polish R. C. Union, Chicago, Ill.
444. Chester Trawinski, Chicago, Ill.
445. Rev. Anthony J. Kolanczyk, Hamtramck, Mich.
452. Casimir Pulaski Wronski, Chicago, Ill.
453. Thaddeus Kosciuszko Wronski, Chicago, Ill.
456. Mrs. Felicia Raczynska, Pittsburgh, Pa.
457. Francis Pawlak, Elmira, N. Y.
467. Rev. Dr. Joseph A. Gierut, Orchard, Lake, Mich.
469. St. Paul's Society, No. 1242, Polish R. C. Union, Thorp, Wis.
477. Adam Dysko, Holyoke, Mass.
484. Rev. John L. Pudlo, Monessen, Pa.
485. Rev. Alexius A. Jarka, Brooklyn, N. Y.
487. Rev. John S. Gulcz, Wilmington, Del.
491. Rev. Andrew Pawelczak, Orchard Lake, Mich.
495. Ladislaus Opalinski, New York, N. Y.
499. Mrs. Bernice Wolnik, Chicago, Ill.
500. Queen Elizabeth Society, No. 1100, Polish R. C. Union, Worcester, Mass.
504. Society of Our Lady of Perpetual Help, No. 156, Polish R. C. Union, Chicago, Ill.
507. Rev. Sister Mary Assumpta, O. S. F., Chicago, Ill.
509. Society of Knights of St. Michael Arch., No. 335, Polish R. C Union, Boswell, Pa.
512. Rev. Miecislaus Mrozinski, Brooklyn, N. Y.
513. Rev. Emil Balutowski, Brooklyn, N. Y.
514. Rev. Ladislaus Galuszka, Brooklyn, N. Y.
515. "Chwalny Panu" Choir, St. Cyril and Methodius Parish, Brooklyn, N. Y.
516. Stanislaus Szostecki, Chicago, Ill.
517. Rev. Sisters of Notre Dame, St. Stanislaus B. M. School, Chicago, Illinois.
522. Gen. Casimir Pulaski Society, No. 491, Polish R. C. Union, Chicago, Ill.
523. St. Stanislaus Society, No. 244, Polish R. C. Union, Philadelphia, Pa.
524. Society of Women of Our Lady of Perpetual Help, No. 448, Polish R. C. Union, Newark, N. J.
526. Fr. Trzeczkowski, Chicago, Ill.
527. Rev. B. J. Dobrzynski, Little Falls, N. Y.
528. Society of Ladies of St. Mary, No. 793, Polish R. C. Union South Bend, Ind.
529. Mrs. Mary Nowicka, Gary, Ind.
531. Holy Trinity Society, No. 337, Polish R. C. Union, Gary, Ind.
532. Hon. Alexander Moc, Chicago, Ill.
537. St. Flizabeth's Society, No. 835, Polish R. C. Union, Pittsburgh, Pa.
538. Joseph Chojnacki, Chicago, Ill.
540. Circuit 73, Polish R. C. Union, Chicago, Ill.
541. St. John the Evangelist Society, No. 394, Polish R. C. Union, Milwaukee, Wis.
543. St. Francis Society, No. 1077, Polish R. C. Union, Detroit, Mich.
547. Francis Harasiuk, Steubenville, Ohio.
549. St. Bronislava Society, No. 1021, Polish R. C. Union, Detroit, Mich.
550. Francis Plocki, Gardner, Mass.
551. Rev. Francis Bolek, Sharon, Pa.
554. Mrs. Rose Wantuch, Chicago, Ill.
561. St. Ann's Society, No. 837, Polish R. C. Union, Chicago, Ill.
562. Joseph J. Ksicinski, Milwaukee, Wis.
568. Peter S. Prazmowski, Jersey City, N. J.
575. Francis Wojcik, Beresford Lake, Man., Canada.
576. Piastic Order of Chivalry, Liverpool, Eng.
577. Hon. John D. Dingell, M. C., Washington, D. C.
578. Mrs. Anna Czaja, Philadelphia, Pa.
579. Rev. Miecislaus Monkiewicz, Philadelphia, Pa.

15

580. Adam Warsza, Chicago. Ill.
581. Hon. Rudolph G. Tenerowicz, M. C., Washington, D. C.
584. Joanna Wojciechowska Erie, Pa.
585. Francis Wojciechowski, Erie, Pa.
586. Mrs. Bronislava Logisz, Chicago, Ill.
587. Joseph Cnota, Chicago. Ill.
589. Society of Polish Women of the Virgin Mary, No. 38, Polish R. C. Union, Chicago, Ill.
590. Francis Gorynski, Sr., Chicago, Ill.
591. Louis M. Zale, Chicago Ill.
592. St. James Society, No. 704, Polish R. C. Union, Chicago, Ill.
594. Edward Babiarz, Chicrgo, Ill.
595. Mrs. Wanda Godzich, Chicago, Ill.
596. Leon Jarosz, Chicago, Ill.
597. Bronislaus A. Jezierski, Boston. Mass.
598. Miss Mary Paryska, Toledo, O.
600. Rev. John Pawelski, Taunton, Minn.
603. Lane Tech High Schoo' Polish Club, Chicago, Ill.
604. Prof. Chester Rondomanski, Syracuse, N. Y.
605. St. Mary of Perpetual Help High School, Chicago, Ill.
606. Thomas Wolanin, Worcester, Mass.
607. Mrs. Bronislava Wolanin, Worcester. Mass.
610. Andrew Bytnar, Chicago, Ill.
611. Polish Book Importing Co., Inc., New York, N. Y.
613. Dr. Alphonse S. Wolarin, Chicago, Ill.
614. Casimir Gonski, Milwaukee, Wis.
615. Guards of Prince J. Pcniatowski, No. 830, Polish R. C. Union, Gardner, Mass.
616. Mrs. Mary Gotowko, Niagara Falls, N. Y.
617. St. Adalbert's B. M. Society, No. 242, Polish R. C. Union, Schenectady, N. Y.
618. St. Peter and Paul Scciety, No. 18, Polish R. C. Union, Chicago, Ill.
619. Society of Our Lady of Gietrzwald. No. 95, Polish R. C. Union, Chester, Pa.
620. Ladislaus Gaska, Binghamton, N. Y.
623. St. Ann's Society, No. 593, Polish R. C. Union, Cicero, Ill.
624. St. Ann's Polish Women Society, No. 265, Polish R. C. Union, Chicago, Ill.
627. Society of St. Therese, No. 722, Polish R. C. Union, Buffalo, New York.
629. Mrs. Martha Zolinska, South Chicago, Ill.
630. Society of the Sacred Heart of Jesus, No. 533, Polish R. C. Union, Chicago, Ill.
631. St. Francis S. Society, No. 371, Polish R. C. Union, Chicago, Ill.
633. St. Ladislaus Society, No. 945, Polish R. C. Union, Hempstend, N. Y.
635. Society of St. Therese, No. 1099, Polish R. C. Union, Chicago, Illinois.
636. St. John's Society, No. 1274, Polish R. C. Union, Chicago, Ill.
637. Rev. Dr. Stanislaus F. Lisewski. Notre Dame, Ind.
638. Boleslaus J. Dalkowski, Toledo, O.
639. Andrew Cieslik, Chicago, Ill.
640. St. Lucy's Society, No. 951, Polish R. C. Union, Depew, N. Y.
641. Society of St. Mary of the Scapulary, No. 810, Polish R. C. Union, Argo, Ill.
642. Rev. W. W. Stancelewski, Newcastle, Pa.
643. St. Stanislaus Kostka Society, No. 149, Polish R. C. Union, Utica, N. Y:
645. St. Valentine's Society, No. 331, Polish R. C. Union, Chicago, Illinois.
649. The Kos Family, West Warwick, R. I.
650. St. John the Baptist Society, No. 792, Polish R. C. Union, Detroit, Mich.
651. Society of Polish Women of St. Apolonia, No. 123, Polish R. C. Union, Chicago, Ill.
652. Peter Bielec, Lowell, Mass.
653. St. Joseph's Society, No. 1163, Polish R. C. Union, Detroit, Mich.

16

655. Very Rev. Mother Mary Scholastica, O. S. F., Buffalo, N. Y
656. St. Joseph's Society, No. 245, Polish R. C. Union, Chicago, Ill.
657. Mrs. Joanna Soberska, Chicago, Ill.
659. Rev. Edward J. Dworaczyk, Panna Maria, Tex.
660. St. Hedwig's Polish Women Society, No. 84, Polish R. C. Union, Cicero, Ill.
661. St. Joseph's Society, No. 1052, Polish R. C. Union, Hinsdale, N. H.
662. Society of St. Therese, No. 1363, Polish R. C. Union, Portland, Conn.
663. Ladislaus P. Starzynski, Chicago, Ill.
664. Miss Frances T. Bisko, Worcester, Mass.
665. Thaddeus T. Wolanin, Worcester, Mass.
666. Francis Sarnecki, Chicago, Ill.
667. Society of Polish Women of St. Rose of Lima, No. 565, Polish R. C. Union, Indiana Harbor, Ind.
668. Polish Arts Club, Chicago, Ill.
669. Mrs. Mary Dyniewicz Kuflewska, Chicago, Ill.
670. Mrs. Kinga Cupryn-Trybus, Chicago, Ill.
671. Mary Klebosita, South Bend, Ind.
672. Society of St. Michael Arch., No. 1029, Polish R. C. Union, Detroit, Mich.
673. Andrew A. Nowak, Bangor, Me.
675. Prof. Dr. Florian Znaniecki, University of Illinois, Urbana, Ill.
677. Peter Salamon, St. Francis, Wis.
678. Rev. Francis X. Kurkowski, Blossburg, Pa.
679. Joseph Widzowski, Syracuse, N. Y.
680. Mrs. Catherine Gryczewska, Chicago, Ill.
681. J. Stephen Zielinski, Chicago, Ill.

POLISH PIONEERS
OF CALIFORNIA

CONTENTS

PREFACE

The purpose of the following paper is to open the pioneer trail through California archives for future historians of the Polish immigration to the State, rather than to give a full and exact account of its beginnings. Owing to distance the author was unable to make a research in local libraries. This will explain, and to some extent, excuse his inaccuracies and errors. The author acknowledges that the gathering of the details contained in this work was made possible only through the kind help given him by the Director, U. S. Coast and Geodetic Survey, Washington, D. C.; California Historical Society, San Francisco; Miss Mabel R. Gillis, State Librarian, California State Library, Sacramento; Mr. Herbert Ingram Priestley, Librarian, The Bancroft Library, Berkeley; Mr. Leslie Edgar Bliss, Librarian, and Mr. Willard O. Waters, Bibliographer for Americana, Henry E. Huntington Library and Art Gallery, San Marino; Miss Lois K. Witherow, Reference Librarian, Stockton Free Public Library; Mr. Stanisław A. Blonski of San Francisco, Cal.; Dr. Bolesław Olszewicz, Librarian, The Joseph Piłsudski University, Warsaw, Poland, and Mr. Louis M. Zale of Chicago. The author's basic studies were conducted at the Newberry Library, Chicago. The Rev. Joseph P. Wachowski of Bay Village, Ohio, revised his manuscript. To all the above institutions and persons the author expresses his sincere thanks.

I.

PORT ROUISSILLON

Nearly a quarter of a century before Jedidiah Strong Smith who was the first to cross the American continent eastward to California, and two scores of years before the beginning of American colonization of that land of gold on a larger scale, the first American vessel sailed into the beautiful bay of Catalina Island, then inhabited by a handful of Indians. It was the *Lelia Byrd,* one of the many ships from New England which the enterprising Yankees used for barter trade between China, California and the United States, ever since the Revolutionary War.

Spanish officials looked with dissatisfied and suspicious eyes on all strangers, but they were usually powerless to prevent their commercial dealings with the few inhabitants of the country. The principal articles of barter were furs of the otter which, now extinct, was very numerous in California at that time. The Americans exported these furs to China and in exchange brought back other valuable goods.

The *Lelia Byrd* just took on a rich cargo of furs in California, but because of her long trip across the Pacific she was forced to undergo some overhauling. Usually, during such lengthy voyages the wooden hulls of vessels accumulated dense layers of weeds which greatly diminished their speed. Worse than that, the weeds became the breeding nests of parasites which ate through the bottom of the vessel. It was necessary to haul the vessel on shore from time to time, and to scrape it and to make needed repairs. This was a dangerous undertaking in continental California. The Spanish officials might detect the vessel and seize it, together with its cargo. To avoid this, the American sailors sought quiet and secluded bays where they could do this unmolested.

Most convenient for this purpose were islands near the shores of California. Captain William Shaler of the *Lelia Byrd* discovered by accident a very suitable spot on Catalina Island, situated about twenty miles from the mainland. On May 1st, 1805, he sailed into the bay, pulled his ship out of the water and made the necessary repairs. And because the bay which served him as a hospitable haven was not yet designated on the world's geography, he named it Port Rouissillon in honor of a Polish exile who accompanied him and Richard Cleveland, supercargo of the vessel, in their voyage.[1]

Who was this Rouissillon?

Before answering this question let us acquaint ourselves with the American friends of the Pole. Shaler and Cleveland were typical merchant-adventurers of New England. They roamed for months and years over the seven seas of the world and bought diverse goods to resell them with profit in some other port.

Once during a voyage from China to Europe they met and became warm companions. Their friendship lasted until their death. Both were not only expert and bold sailors, but also men of noble souls. Many years later Shaler became consul general of the United States in Algiers. Transferred as consul to Havana, he engaged Cleveland as his vice-consul and evenly divided all his income with him.

The diaries which both of them left attest to their high intelligence. Quite popular many decades ago, especially the diary of Cleveland, their writings still are interesting documents in connection with the history of early California and old American merchant marine.

Soon after their first meeting the young New Englanders decided to make together a

---

[1] Robert G. Cleland, **A History of California, The American Period,** New York, 1912, p. p. 13 and 470; Mrs. M. Burton Williamson, "History of Santa Catalina Island," **Publications of the Historical Society of Southern California,** Los Angeles, vol. VI, 1903-5, p. 20.

voyage to the western shores of America and, should good luck attend them, a trip around the world. Having sold advantageously their cargo of coffee brought to Copenhagen, they set out to Hamburg to purchase a new vessel. They choose and bought the *Lelia Byrd* of American registry: the ship was of 175 tons, comfortable, spacious and strong.

It was during their stay at Hamburg that they met Rouissillon. He was then 28 years old. Both were so satisfied with their new Polish friend that they invited him to accompany them. Cleveland tells about this episode in his interesting diary:

"During sojourn at Hamburg, we had become acquainted with the count de Rouissillon, a young Polish nobleman of superior education and talents. He had fought for the liberty of his country, as aide-de-camp to the unfortunate Kosciuszko; and being one of the proscribed, was living in Hamburg on slender means, and without occupation. In the society of a gentleman of such intelligence, accomplishments, and companionable traits, we knew that we should be repaid for the additional expense of taking him as compagnon de voyage, and we agreed to invite him to accompany us as such. He had never been at sea, and a voyage round the world to a man like him, reared in the interior of a continent, offered much attractions that he acceded to the proposal not only without hesitation, but with expressions of great satisfaction and delight." 2

They loaded their vessel with various goods and sailed from Cuxhaven on November 8th, 1801. By drawing lots, Shaler became captain and Cleveland supercargo of the ship. Her crew numbered nine men besides them.

2Richard Jeffry Cleveland, **A Narrative of Voyages and Commercial Enterprizes**, Cambridge, 1843, p. 156.

At Canary Islands they made a stop to re-provision the vessel and on January 2nd, 1802, reached Rio Janeiro. There the three friends visited a Benedictine monastery where they admired a magnificent library and where Cleveland's and Shaler's love of books and Rouissillon's knowledge of literature was, in turn, admired by the monks.

Rounding Cape Horn, they sailed into the harbor of Valparaiso, on February 24th, 1802. There they experienced many indignities from Spanish officials, and even were imprisoned as suspects intending to infringe on the Spanish trade monopoly. Rouissillon did what he could to help his friends in these troubles. After long legal quarrels and many annoyances they were able to leave the inhospitable port not sooner, however, than the middle of May. They directed their course toward Galapagos Islands where they rested for a week amid the beauties of nature. Leaving the islands they reached San Blas, in Mexico. on July 11th, 1802.

There they met with new difficulties raised by local Spanish authorities. Rouissillon now had an opportunity to repay the good Americans for their kindness. Going to the Governor at Tipec, and later to the Viceroy at Mexico City, he, after many weeks of endeavors, received permission for them to remain in the port and to dispose of their wares with profit. Indeed, they sold their cargo for $10,000, and were able to reprovision their ship and to buy cheaply 1,600 otter skins, freshly imported from California.

At San Blas Rouissillon separated from the Americans. The Pole wished to remain in Mexico for some time in order to acquaint himself with that interesting country, the seat of an ancient culture, and then to pass on to the United States where he hoped to rejoin his old friends and to spend the rest of his life in an atmosphere of liberty.

The Americans liked Rouissillon, and he, in turn, became much attached to them. Cleveland did not try to conceal his feelings when writing in his memoir of their parting:

"It was with feelings of deep regret, that we parted here, with our excellent and amiable friend the Count John de Rouissillon, with whom we had been so intimately associated for so long a period, and who had shared so largely in the various perplexing scenes, incident to the persecution of our object. To his address and perseverance we were mainly indebted for the permission obtained from the Viceroy of Mexico for the sale of a part of our cargo; and for the indulgence of the additional time in port, necessary to secure the sea otters' skins. We had left with him, manufactures to the amount of about $3,000 cost; and which were worth, at the actual prices there, more than three times that cost. From the proceeds of this, after defraying his expenses, he was to account with us in the United States, where we anticipated much pleasure in meeting him, in the course of ensuing year. At parting, he expressed the unalloyed enjoyment he had experienced on board, his grateful feelings for our confidence, and his earnest desire of realizing the pleasure of meeting us again in that land of liberty and of equal rights, of which, he said, he should be proud to become a citizen.

"The Count de Rouissillon" continues Cleveland, "was the descendant of an ancient noble family of Poland. An advocate for liberty, he could not brook the subjugation of his country; and for his efforts to avert it, he was proscribed, and was without a home when we became acquainted with him at Hamburg. He possessed a powerful intellect, and gave evidence, that great care had been taken in its cultivation. His acquirements in mathematics, in astronomy, in music, in drawing, were very respectable, and there was scarcely a European language with which he was not familiar. Having with him among others, books in the Russian, Polish and German languages, the Spanish authorities, who are extremely watchful and vigorous in their examination of all books, were actually confounded by them; but allowed them to pass on the well-grounded conviction, that nobody in the country could read them, and therefore, that they could do no harm. For these attainments he was not more indebted to a fine intellect than to an untiring industry, which was so habitual, that he seemed to grudge a moment's time that was passed without adding something to his knowledge. So that when walking the deck for exercise, if there was nobody to walk and converse with him, he would be engaged in practising some new music on his flute. Being at this time only 28 years of age, his prospect for honorable distinction seemed all that his ambition could desire: but unfortunately, his earthly course was cut short not long after we parted. To our great grief we learned, on arriving in the United States, that he died in Mexico some time in the year 1803. The exclusive policy of the Spanish government, relating to all foreigners, then in full operation, made it so difficult to obtain any information from Mexico, that we were discouraged from any attempt to ascertain the particulars of his death, or to learn what became of our property, or of his effects: and to this day, we remain in ignorance of everything relating to these subjects."[3]

Not only Cleveland, but evidently Shaler also became attached to the Pole. Mentioning the bay of the island he said in his diary: "As I was the first navigator who had ever visited and surveyed this place, I took the liberty of naming it after my much respected friend, M. de Rouissillon."[4]

---

[3]Ib., p. p. 203-5.
[4]William Shaler, "Journal of a Voyage from China to the Southwestern Coast of America made in 1804," American Register, vol. II, 1808, p. p. 148.

Bancroft calls Rouissillon "a distinguished Pole",[5] and Cleveland's son who undoubtedly heard much from his father about the stranger devotes this paragraph to the three friends:

"The fact of their (Cleveland's and Shaler's) winning the friendship of so accomplished a man as the Count de Rouissillon, the mutual appreciation of the value of the intellectual enjoyment of each other's society which was manifested by the invitation and its acceptance, and the subsequent relations of harmony and confidence which were maintained between the three throughout the extended period of trying experiences to which they were subjected, afford evidences of such characteristics in each as can but excite surprise and admiration, and serve to lift the whole enterprise above the domain of a mere trading voyage, and impart to it a halo of attractive interest which may be justly termed poetic."[6]

Indeed, there was a touch of poetry in this little episode in the history of the old American sea voyages. But all these particulars do not solve the riddle of John, Count de Rouissillon's identity. Polish heraldry books do not contain such a name in their lists of Polish nobles. Nor can it be found among the aides-de-camp of General Kosciuszko during his Insurrection of 1794. It may only be surmised that Rouissillon was not the man's real name, and that he lived at Hamburg under an assumed one in order to escape the vengeance of his country's enemies.

Rouissillon's name did not survive in California's geography. The port is now called Avalon and is a modern resort. Its former name is

---

[5]Hubert H. Bancroft, History of California, San Francisco, vol. II, p. p. 11-12.

[6]H. W. S. Cleveland, Voyages of a Merchant Navigator of the Days that are past, compiled from the Journals and Letters of the late Richard Jeffry Cleveland, New York, 1886 p. 74.

in any event, the first, though indirect, connecting-link between California and the Polish immigration, while the mysterious Polish Count still lives in history as a participant of one of the first American voyages to that country.

II.

POLES AMONG THE RUSSIANS IN ALASKA
AND CALIFORNIA

Chronologically, the next Polish traces in California should be sought in the history of the Russian efforts to colonize it.

In 1811, the Russians, ignoring the vain protests of the Spaniards, founded a colony of their own on the Bodega Bay, near the present city of San Francisco. To protect it, they built Fort Ross. This was a continuation of the rapacious policy of Peter the Great and of Catharine II. After absorbing what she could in Europe and Asia, Russia now turned her eyes to America where she already possessed Alaska. Fort Ross was intended to be only the first step toward seizing the whole of California and Oregon and founding of a great Russian-American empire. The colony was to secure for her the lucrative trade in otter skins, and also to be a source of food stuffs for the barren and cold territory of Alaska. In 1822, Tsar Alexander I issued an ukase which was a step further toward that goal as it closed the northern Pacific to all vessels, except Russian. President Monroe of the United States answered it by promulgating his famous doctrine. During the next few years the trade in otter skins lost its significance and no political event occurred which would give Russia a pretext to separate California from Spain by force. Moreover, Russia's attention became occupied more by European events. Gradually the St. Petersburg government lost its interest in the American colonization and in 1840, it sold Fort Ross to John A. Sutter, a Swiss, who organized there what amounted to a little principality of his own.

The Russian colony in California never was very populous. In about 1840, there lived some four hundred people in and around Fort Ross: of these only sixty were whites and eighty Kodiaks,[7] and the rest were Indians.

It is almost certain that Poles came in contact with the Russian colony in California during nearly thirty years of its existence. The first Poles appeared in Alaska in the 18th century and undoubtedly from there they came to Fort Ross, as Russian vessels kept up a steady communication between the two colonies.

The part played by the Poles in the Russian expeditions to Alaska and in its colonization deserves to be the subject of a special study. It is worth while, however, to mention here that already in Bering's and Chirikoff's expeditions of 1740-41, which brought about the discovery of Alaska, we find Polish names among the members of their crews. Such were, for instance, Cadet Andreas Velikopolski (Wielkopolski) and ship carpenters Andreas Kozmin and Wilhelm Butzovski (Buczowski) who accompanied Bering,[8] Peter the Great recruited many members of this expedition from among the foreigners as there were no Russians suited for the task. It is also known that Maurice August Beniowski, the famous adventurer, fleeing from Siberia aboard a captured vessel, appeared near Alaska's shores in 1771, some years before the founding of the first Russian settlements. He was accompanied by Casimir Bielski, a former member of the Confederacy of Bar.[9] It is known further that in 1807, two Polish exiles, Leszczynski and Berezowski, lived in New Archangelsk, in Alaska; most probably there were also other Polish exiles.[10]

Some of them evidently married local women, as a certain Klimovsky (Klimowski), whose son Andreas, born in Alaska (died in 1831), was a ship's captain.[11] Aboard the *Suworoff*, a Rus-

---

[7] Inhabitants of Kodiak Island, near Alaska.
[8] Hubert H. Bancroft, **History of Alaska,** San Francisco, 1890. p. 93.
[9] Ib., p. 179.
[10] Ib., p. 464.
[11] Ib., p. 438.

sian man-of-war, which arrived at New Archangelsk after a voyage of more than one year from Kronstadt in 1814, there were Lieutenants Schveikovsky (Szwejkowski)) and Semion Yanovski (Janowski);[12] Yanovski, together with Korsakovsky (Korsakowski) led a scientific expedition into the interior of Alaska in 1818.[13] and in 1821, was appointed Governor of Russian America;[14] though russianized, undoubtedly he was of Polish descent. These are only a few facts taken at random, but all pointing to a quite significant role which the Poles played in the early history of Alaska, and, incidentally, of California.

The sea, besides hunting, was practically the only sphere of labor in Alaska, and, naturally, Polish names may also be found among Alaskan sea captains. They were, perhaps like Klimowski, born and reared in Alaska, but with more or less Polish blood in their veins.

One of them especially, Dionisius Zaremba, is often mentioned in the annals of California. He frequently visited Fort Ross since 1827, when he appeared for the first time as captain of the brig *Okhotsk*. In 1831, he put into Bodega bay as commander of the bark *Urup*. About 1845 he was sent to California as an agent of the Russian American Company to liquidate affairs connected with the sale of Fort Ross to Sutter.[15] One of the islands near the southwestern coast of Alaska bears his name to this day.

Another Alaskan sea captain who visited California in 1839-40, and whose name seems of Polish origin, was Stephen Vallivode (Waliwoda) of *Elena*. [16]

---

[12]Ib., p. 504.

[13]Ib., p. p. 511, 521-2.

[14]The Russians in California, San Francisco, California Historical Society, 1933, p. 46; California Historical Society Quarterly, vol. XII, 1933, p. 234.

[15]William Heath Davis, Seventy Five Years in California, San Francisco, 1929, p. 402; Bancroft, History of California, vol. III, p. p. 148, 213, 384; vol. IV. p. p. 187-8.

[16]Bancroft, History of California, vol. V, p. 759.

III

POLES AMONG THE AMERICAN
IMMIGRANTS BEFORE 1849

Outside of Fort Ross there were probably no Poles in California until the beginning of the American immigration in 1841. Of course, Americans lived in California some years before that date, but in a very small number. They settled there, despite the prohibition, at first of the Spanish, and later of the Mexican laws, ever since foreign merchant vessels began to appear on California shores. American trappers appeared in California, coming by land, as early as 1826, but this was a receding influx; the purpose of their expeditions was hunting, not settlement. Up to 1841, several hundred Americans reached California, but at that time only about fifty of them were permanently settled there.

In the beginning of the fifth decade of the past century the frontier of the United States extended westwardly not far beyond the Mississippi. The "Wild West" was rather unknown. Narratives of trappers who visited the new land excited the fantasy of frontiersmen who always liked unlimited freedom and were ever ready to look for it in new surroundings.

The years of 1839-41 were years of depression in the country and this to a great extent, influenced emigration toward the west. The movement culminated in 1841. The prospective emigrants from states east of the Mississippi organized their own companies, sold their belongings and made ready for the long journey. Sapling Grove, Kas., was chosen as the meeting point of the earliest group of these emigrants.

But, though there were many willing, few were bold enough to risk the long and dangerous jorney into the unknown. Most of the volunteers backed down, and only 48 emigrants, with 15 women and children, from Missouri and Arkansas, appeared at the meeting point.

At their camp on the Kansas River the emigrants elected John Bartleson their leader and on May 19th, 1841, they started their long trek through the present states of Kansas, Colorado, Utah and Nevada. The pioneers underwent severe hardships. Many times they were threatened by death. Hunger and sickness became their companions. When they reached the Walker River in the middle of October, they all were utterly exhausted and still the high and difficult to pass Sierras divided them from California.

It took two weeks to cross the mountains in a southwestern direction. Their oxen fell on the way, or were eaten and their mules became their only food. Some of the wanderers lost their lives in the snows and precipices of the Sierras. The boldest abandoned the hope of ever reaching California, the strongest were sick and discouraged. When the despair of the ragged and emaciated band reached its climax, suddenly the beautiful and green valley of the Stanislaus River[17] loomed up before their eyes. Their dreadful journey lasted five and a half months, but now they had reached the threshold of the "promised land."

Henry Lyons Brolaski

Among these brave pioneers was Henry Lyons Brolaski (Brolaskey) of St. Louis, undoubtedly of Polish origin or descent.[18] When Josiah Belden began to recruit the volunteers for

---

[17]This is another early Polish geographical name in California. Besides the river, there are mountains, a peak (Alpine County), a town (Tuolomne County), and a county which bear the name of Stanislaus. They were so named after Stanislaus, or Estanislao, an Indian of the Wallawalla tribe, who led uprisings against Mexican authorities in the first half of the past century.

[18]He belonged to a family which lived in America for a considerable time. J. H. Brolaski of Pennsylvania was American consul at Jerusalem, Palestine, in 1849-52.

the journey, Brolaski joined him and appeared at Sapling Grove. He overcame all hardships and reached California safely. Notwithstanding all the restrictions imposed on foreigners by the Mexican authorities, the emigrants were well received by the Californians; they dispersed through the land, and Brolaski settled at Monterey, where he lived for a year.[19] He was probably the first American Pole to reach California by the continental route.

Stanislaus Pongowski

The next Pole of whose presence in the state we possess certain knowledge, was Stanislaus Pongowski (Pągowski). He appeared there about 1843, coming by sea from Australia. Born in Courland[20] in 1800, as a member of a prominent Polish noble family, he chose a military career and became aide-de-camp to General Vincent Krasinski, father of one of the famous trio of Polish romantic poets. He took part in the Polish Insurrection against Russia of 1830-1, advanced to the rank of Major and won the cross of Virtuti Militari. After the suppression of the movement he lived as an exile in France, Tunisia, Turkey, England, and finally in Australia, constantly changing places with the uneasiness which characterized the "Great Emigration" of Polish patriots of that period. No details are known of his stay in California, but he did not find peace

---

[19]Bancroft, **History of California**, vol. II, p. 731. Brolaski· soon left California and in 1844, appeared at Callao, Peru, where he inherited some business from his brother, which he conducted for a few years. In September of 1848, he returned to St. Louis. Bancroft notes that after the discovery of gold he intended to return to California, but expresses doubt whether he was among the "Forty-Niners." A H. S. Brolaski, undoubtedly the same individual, appears, however, on the list of "Forty-Niners" in the **Argonauts of California** (by a Pioneer, New York, 1890, p. 402) as a member of the Haviland Mining Co. of New Orleans.

[20]Now Latvia.

even there and emigrated to Chile where he finally settled for good and became a prominent citizen.21

In 1845, Francis (Francisco) Surok (or Syrec) appeared in California; in 1849, he was proprietor of a store on the Moquelumne River.22 Another early Polish California pioneer was Albert Pulaski (or Pollasky) who came in 1846 and often stayed at Fort Ross which John Sutter renamed New Helvetia. As New Helvetia became a station for immigrants coming by the continental route, most probably Pulaski also came to California by land. Marcus Pollasky founded the town of Pollasky on the San Joaquin River, Fresno County, still existing as Friant today. He was a railroad promoter and early planned a transcontinental line across the Sierras. A northeast branch of the Southern Pacific Railroad still bears the name Pollasky Road.23

Dr. Felix Paul Wierzbicki

In the spring of 1847, Doctor Felix Paul Wierzbicki, the most famous Polish pioneer of California, arrived with the regiment of Colonel J. D. Stevenson.

21Rocznik Towarzystwa Historyczno-Literackiego w Paryżu, Paris, 1867, p. p. 395-6. In 1864, Pongowski returned from Chile to Poland to take part in a new uprising, the January Insurrection, but was arrested by the Russians and sentenced to fifteen years of hard labor; with greatest difficulty he regained his freedom and died on the return way to Chile.

22Bancroft, History of California, vol. V, p. 741.

23Ib., vol. IV, p. 785; Paul E. Vandor, History of Fresno County, Cal., Los Angeles, 1919, vol. I. p. p. 272 and 282. A. Pollaski was later a member of the Pioneers' Society of Sacramento (The Argonauts of California, p. 376.) Quite frequently mentioned by sources is Louis Polaski, an early merchant of Los Angeles and Monterey (Harris Newmark, Sixty Years in Southern California, 1853-1913, New York, 1916, p. 70; J. A. Graves, My Seventy Years in California, 1857-1927, Los Angeles, 1927, p. p. 91-2, 109-10; William H. Knight, Handbook Almanac for the Pacific States, San Francisco, 1863, p. 180).

He was born at Czerniawka, a village in the Polish province of Volhynia, on January 1st, 1815. As a boy of 15 years he took part in the November Insurrection of 1830-1. Arrested by the Austrian authorities, he was deported to the United States together with 234 other Polish officers and soldiers, in 1834.

Courtesy of the University of California Hospital, San Francisco, Cal.
Photo by Casimir K. Blonski, San Francisco, Cal.

DR. FELIX PAUL WIERZBICKI

Part of a mural showing the history of medicine in California, by Bernard Zakheim and Phyllis Wrightson, in Toland Hall, University of California Hospital, San Francisco, Cal.

The early lot of these exiles in this country was full of hardships, but Wierzbicki was lucky enough to find a philanthropic American family who helped him to finish his education. It is known that for some time he taught French privately in the East, and then became a doctor of medicine and practiced it at Providence, R. I. In 1841, he published under a pseudonym of Philokalist, a philosophical treatise *The Ideal Man*,24 and in 1846, a series of articles on the history of Poland in *The American Whig Review*.25

When Col. Jonathan D. Stevenson began to recruit his regiment at New York for the service in California during the war with Mexico, Wierzbicki enlisted as a volunteer. All commissions were disposed of and he had to be satisfied with the grade of sergeant of Company F, but was promised to receive surgeon's rank in case of a vacancy. When after a long journey the little flotilla bearing the regiment reached San Francisco, Stevenson broke his promise and ignored Wierzbicki in filling a vacant place in the medical service. Wierzbicki appealed to Gen. Kearny and requested to be discharged. Evidently recognizing the justice of his grievance Kearny discharged him honorably on April 28, 1847. Wierzbicki later attained the rank of Assistant Surgeon, U. S. Army, his second discharge being dated November 24, 1855.

Besides becoming a pioneer physician of San Francisco, Wierzbicki immediately began to take a lively part in the public life of the little city. This gave him a chance to befriend Mariano Guadalupe Vallejo, the eminent Mexican leader; Ferdinand C. Ewer whom he accidentally helped to become editor of the *Pacific News*,26 and other prominent men. On June 26, 1847, he acquired several city lots which may be taken as a proof

---

24The Ideal Man; a Conversation between two Friends upon the Beautiful, the Good, the True, as Manifested in Actual Life, Boston, 1841.

25"Three Chapters on the History of Poland," The American Whig Review, New York, vol. III, p. p. 488 and 631; vol. IV, p. 45; and an additional article "Brighter Days for Poland," ib., vol. IV, p. 188.

26Henry Ramp Wagner, "The Life of Ferdinand C. Ewer," California Historical Society Quarterly, vol. XIII, Dec. 1934, No. 4, p. 296-7; vol. XIV, March 1935, No. 1, p. 78.

of his early intention to settle in the country permanently.[27]

When in January of 1848 California was electrified by the news of the discovery of gold, Wierzbicki, as may be assumed from his writings, did not become much enthusiastic over the fact. "All other mines are more beneficent in their influence to the progress of a country than gold mines", wrote he in his *California*.[28] Nevertheless, he made a four months tour through the Gold Region. On foot and horse he visited nearly the whole state, through its length and width and even crossed the Sierras and reached the borders of the great Western Desert.

The result of his travels was a pamphlet *California as it is, and as it may be, or a Guide to the Gold Region,* "probably the most important book that was ever printed in California."[29] It was not only the first English book printed at San Francisco and west of the Rockies, but also a very good description of the state during the important period of the Gold Rush. In its original two editions, it is a bibliographical rarity, valued at more than its weight in gold.[30]

Wierzbicki became also a pioneer member of the Medical Society of the State of California, and published the first article on the history of

---

[27]Commissioners to Enquire on the City Property, **Report on the Condition of the Real Estate within the Limits of the City of San Francisco,** San Francisco, January, 1851, p. 110. The lots were Nos. 671, 672, 684 and 685, all of 50 vara (rods).

[28]**The Magazine of History,** Tarrytown, vol. XXXII, No. 2, p. 66.

[29]Henry Ramp Wagner, **California Imprints, Augu**st **1846 — June 1851,** Berkeley, 1922, p. p. 24-5.

[30]Probably the earliest Californiana in the Polish language is a series of essays "Kilka Słów o Kalifornji" (A few Remarks on California) and "O Złocie" (Gold) by John Mitkiewicz (1804-1866), printed in the **Biblioteka Warszawska,** vol. II, No. 1, in 1849. It is not known when, or whether at all, Mitkiewicz visited California. For his biography see Stanislaw Zieliński, **Mały Słownik Pionierów Polskich,** Warszawa, 1932, p. 669.

medicine in the state.[31] He died on December 26, 1860, at San Francisco and was buried there in the Laurel Hill Cemetery.[32]

WIERZBICKI'S GRAVE

Presidio National Cemetery, San Francisco

Dr. Wierzbicki's services to the state are commemorated by a mural now adorning the Toland Hall, University of California Hospital, San Francisco; it is the work of Bernard Zakheim and Phyllis Wrightson.

Other immigrants before 1849

Was Dr. Wierzbicki the only Pole in Stevenson's regiment? Its roster contains several other supposedly P o l i s h names; they are:

Ernest F. Dunitch, musician

John Hommitch, private, Company K.

Joseph Luskey, p r i v a t e, Company A.

Charles Zetschsky, private, Company C.[33]

To this regiment also belonged the whole family of Emmanuel Charles Christin Russ who was of Polish descent, though born in Germany.

---

[31]"Essay on History of Medicine", **California State Journal of Medicine,** San Francisco, vol. I, 1856, p. 147.

[32]An excellent biography of Wierzbicki by Dr. George D. Lyman "Wierzbicki, The Book and the Doctor", may be found as introduction to the reprint of **California as it is** by the Grabborn Press, San Francisco, 1933, (bibliography given). See also: Mieczysław Haiman, **Feliks Paweł Wierzbicki i jego "California",** Chicago, 1933; Stanisław Zieliński, **Mały Słownik Pionierów Polskich,** p. 592; (with bibliography); B. Bolesławita, **Rachunki z Roku** 1867, Poznań, 1868, vol. II, p. 98-9; S. Austin Allibone, **A Critical Dictionary of English Literature and British and American Authors,** London, 1897, vol. III, p. 2709.

[33]A Pioneer, **The Argonauts of California,** p. 394; Bancroft, **History of California,** vol. II, p. p. 784 and 787.

He immigrated to America in 1832 and together with his older son enlisted as privates, while his younger sons were drummer, and trumpeter respectively in the regiment, and his wife and four daughters served as sutlers and servants.[34]

After landing in California Hommitch with his Company was stationed at San Francisco presidio; the Company of Zetschsky was sent to Soncma; and that of Luskey to Santa Barbara. Dunitch still lived at Placerville, Cal., in 1883. The family of Russ attained prominence and wealth in the state.

By the end of 1848, four companies of dragoons of the United States Army, under Major Graham, arrived after taking part in the Mexican War and after a difficult march of three months from Coahuila, through Chihuahua and Tucson. To this expedition belonged Jacob Rogenade from Poland, who, in 1854, fell victim of a murder at Los Angeles.[35]

---

[34]W. F. Swasey, **The Early Days and Men of California,** Oakland, 1891, p. p. 229-239.

[35]Bancroft, **History of California,** vol. V, p. 702.

IV.
POLISH FORTY-NINERS

The Gold Rush lured swarms of immigrants from all parts of the world to California and also increased the number of Poles. Several contemporary authors note their presence generally.[36] Among the Babel of tongues one could overhear the Polish language occasionally; a Pole or two could be found everywhere. They came to California by the sea around the Cape Horn, or through Panama, or, eventually, over land, braving all the dangers and hardships of the long journey. In the spring of 1849 about 50,000 persons were trudging by land to California and another 50,000 hurried there by the two other routes.

The most important among Polish Forty-Niners were:

Captain Rudolph Korwin Piotrowski.

Rudolph K. Piotrowski came to California as a member of the Pittsburgh Enterprise Company which started its long trek across the country on April 13th, 1849.[37] Born in Kamien, in the old Palatinate of Lublin, in 1814, he played an enthusiastic part in the Polish November Insurrection of 1830-1 against Russia. He distinguished himself signally in several battles and advanced to the rank of Captain of Uhlans, winning also

---

[36]Ernest de Massey, "A Frenchman in the Gold Rush", **California Historical Society Publications,** San Francisco, 1927, p. 15; Alexandre Holinski, **La California et les Routes Interoceaniques,** Bruxelles, 1853, p. 167; Frank Soule, John H. Gilson and James Nisbet, **The Annals of San Francisco,** New York, 1855, p. p. 412 and 667; Kalixt Wolski, **Do Ameryki i w Ameryce,** Lwów, 1877, p. 385.

[37]A Pioneer, **The Argonauts of California,** p. p. 369 and 400. Bancroft mentions him as a member of the San Francisco Pioneers' society though gives a wrong date of his arrival in California. (**History of California,** vol. IV, p. p. 453, 772, 775, 781).

the highly prized *Virtuti Militari* cross for his bravery.

After the Insurrection became a lost cause he emigrated with many other patriots to France and there married a French woman, but not too happily. In 1840, he came to the United States and for a while led a rather nomadic life. In 1848, he is listed as a member of the Polish Committee at New Orleans, La.[38]

He began life in California as a gold miner. From his savings he was able to buy some land near San Francisco where he founded the town of Sebastopol; undoubtedly the Captain chose that name to celebrate the capture of the Russian fortress Sevastopol by the allied forces in the Crimean War.

Democratic to the core, he was an enthusiastic supporter of the Union during the Civil War. Among his intimate American friends were Newton Booth, Governor of the State and United States Senator, and Booth's successor in the governorship, Romualdo Pacheco. There is no doubt that Piotrowski was the Captain of Booth's short story "After Dark", mostly dealing with prominent Poles in France.[39] He was also very popular among the Poles and was one of the founders of the Polish Society of California. He liberally contributed to all worthy purposes and he was one of those who helped Helena Modjeska, the famous Shakespearean actress, in the beginning of her spectacular American career. The actress left a very interesting sketch of him in her writings.[40] Henry Sienkiewicz, whom he also met and befriended, immortalized him as Zagloba in his famous novel *With Fire and Sword*.

[38]B. Bolesławita, **Rachunki z Roku 1867**, Poznań, 1868, vol. II, p. 114; **Kuryer Warszawski**, 1883, No. 126.

[39]Lauren E. Crane, ed., **Newton Booth of California, His Speeches and Addresses**, New York and London, 1894, p. p. 463-75.

[40]Helena Modjeska, **Memories and Impressions**, New York, 1910, p. p. 269-303.

A few years before his death he lost his sight and feeling his end nearing, returned to France in order to die as near Poland as possible. He lived a few more years in the Polish Institute of St. Casimir at Paris and died there in 1883.[41]

Doctor John Strentzel.

Another very prominent Polish Forty-Niner was Dr. John Strentzel, a physician and a veteran of the Polish November Insurrection of 1830-1. He arrived in this country in 1840 and became a pioneer settler on the present site of the city of Dallas, Texas, which was then a wild Comanche country. He lived later in Lamar County, Texas, and in 1849, with his wife and a small daughter left for California by land, attached as a surgeon to a group of emigrants. Soon he settled in the Alhambra Valley which he named after Irving's glowing description of the Moorish paradise.

Dr. Strentzel was a very successful pioneer horticulturist of California. He died suddenly on October 21, 1890.

His daughter, Louie Wanda Strentzel, married John Muir, the famous naturalist, and the Strentzel ranch in Alhambra became their lifelong residence. Mrs. Muir brought great happiness into the life of her gifted husband; he found in her a lifelong friend and an understanding companion of his labors. Her death on August 6th, 1905, was a great shock to him.[42]

---

[41]Ks. A. Syski, **Zakład św. Kazimierza w Paryżu**, Warszawa, Łuck, 1936, p. 251. Brief biographical sketches of Piotrowski may also be found in Agaton Giller's **Album Muzeum Narodowego w Rapperswylu, Wieniec Pamiątkowy**, Rapperswyl, 1881, p. p. 480-1, and in Zielinski's **Mały Słownik Pionierow Polskich**, p. 366.

[42]William Frederick Bade, **The Life and Letters of John Muir**, Boston and New York, 1924, vol. II, index; **California Historical Society Quarterly**, vol. IV, 1925, p. 295; Hieronim Kunaszowski, **życiorysy Uczestników Powstania Listopadowego**, Lwów, 1880, p. 151.

Captain Alexander Zakrzewski

A notable Forty-Niner without doubt was Alexander Zakrzewski, a former officer of the army which fought for Poland's freedom in the November Insurrection. Among the records of Clackamas County, at Oregon City, Oregon, there is in the state of perfect preservation one of the oldest plans of San Francisco drawn by him.

Drawn by A. Zakrzewski, Courtesy of the Henry E. Hungtington Library and Art Gallery, San Marino, Cal.

ZAKRZEWSKI'S "TOPOGRA-PHICAL OFFICE,"
SAN FRANCISCO

Washington and Montgomery sts. (From his "Map of San Francisco" of 1854)

This map in on wax paper, 18x22 inches; its edges are framed with a green silk band. The drawing is fine and accurate. The map contains 1,539 lots, divided by streets and squares, north-west of the present Market street, the city's former main artery, and 700 lots southwest of it. Its full title is: "Official Map of San Francisco, Completed from the field notes of the official re-survey made by Wm. M. Eddy, C. E., Surveyor of the town of San Francisco. Drawn by Alexander Zakrzewski, Ex-Polish Officer, 1849."

Because of a sudden influx of gold seekers, San Francisco grew by leaps and bounds. During the first months of 1849, about 10,000 persons came into the city, and about 30,000 more arrived in the second half of that year. The old city boundaries were not spacious enough to accommodate the influx. All city lots surveyed formerly were sold out. Consequently Mayor J. W. Geary on taking office in August 1849, ordered Eddy to widen the survey on additional land up

to the present Larkin and Eighth Streets.43 Zakrzewski helped Eddy in this survey and afterwards made the above mentioned map.44

Alexander Zakrzewski was born on January
1, 1799, at Sandomierz, in Poland, and received an
education as a military engineer. In 1825, he became Second Lieutenant of Engineers in the Polish army, took an active part in the November
Uprising of 1830-1, and advanced to the rank of
Captain.He was an able lithographer and published
several maps at Warsaw. After the insurrection
was suppressed he emigrated to France with the
remnants of the Polish army. While in Paris he
made some engravings. He later led a wandering
life, living for some time in Tahiti, Madagascar
and Reunion Islands, till finally he came to California, undoubtedly with one of the first groups of
FortyNiners.45 On November 28th, 1849, he was
granted a city lot No. 1172, of 50 vara. 46

Besides the aforementioned map, Captain
Zakrzewski made also several other early maps of
San Francisco.47 He is listed as a lithographer in
San Francisco's first city directory of 1850 and
at that time lived on Clay street, between Dupont

43Bancroft, **History of California**, vol. VI, p. 194.

44See: Anthony W. Vogdes, **A Bibliography relating
to the Geology, Paleontology, and Mineral Resources of
California**, Bulletin No. 30 of the California State Mining
Bureau, Sacramento, 1904, p. p. 231-2. Surveys had to be
approved by the federal Land Office and the only such
office in the Far West at that time was at Oregon City;
this is the reason why Zakrzewski's map is deposited
there.

45Bolesław Olszewicz, **Polska Kartografia Wojskowa**,
Warszawa, 1921, p. p. 138, 142-3.

46Commissioners to enquire into city property, **Report
on the Condition** . . . etc., p. 134.

47Some of them are: **Plan of San Francisco from the
Official-Map in the Surveyor's Office. Reduced and Drawn
by Alexa. Zakrzewski, Ex-Polish Officer, 1850** (in pen and
ink, in the collection of the Society of California Pioneers,
San Francisco); **Complete Map of San Francisco. Compiled
from the original map, the recent surveys of W. M. Eddy,
County Surveyor, also the Western Addition surveyed by
S. K. Marlette, C. E. Containing all the latest extensions**

and Kearny.[48] His map of 1854 gives his address at the corner of Washington and Montgomery streets. In 1857, he published a map of Arizona. In 1859, or probably much earlier, he occupied the position of a draughtsman in the United States Surveyor-General's Office at San Francisco, with a yearly salary of $2,000.[49]

Sometime in 1850, "Zakreski and Hartman" made a lithograph entitled: "View of the Procession in Celebration of the Admission of California, Oct. 29th, 1850," after the drawing by J.

---

and improvements, new streets, alleys, etc. Respectfully dedicated to the citizens of San Francisco by Alex. Zakresi and Hartman, lithographers, 1851. Published by S. K. Marlette, C. E., and by Alex. Zakresi and Hartman (University of California, Library Bulletin No. 9. List of Printed Maps of California, Berkeley, 1887, p. 18; Vogdes, op. cit.); A Topographical and complete Map of San Francisco. Compiled from the Original Map, from the recent Surveys of W. M. Eddy, County Surveyor, and others, containing all the latest extensions and improvements, new streets, alleys, places, wharves, etc. Respectfully dedicated to the citizens of San Francisco, 1853. Lith. by Alex. Zareski and Co. For Sale by Cooks, Lenny and Co., San Francisco (California Historical Society, San Francisco; Univ. of Cal., Library Bulletin No. 9, p. 19; Vogdes, op. cit.; Harry T. Peters, California on Stone, New York, 1935, p. p. 205-6); The only correct and fully complete Map of San Francisco. Compiled from the Original Map and recent Surveys. Containing all the extensions and improvements, new streets, places, wharves and divisions of wards. Respectfully Dedicated to the City Authorities, by Alex. Zakreski, 1853. Drawn and Lithographed by Alex. Zakreski etc . . . (Henry E. Huntington Library and Art Gallery, San Marino; Peters, op. cit.); the last mentioned map was also issued by Zakrzewski in 1852 and 1854. the latter having marginal views of public buildings at San Francisco: Plan of Marysville compiled from the original map. Respectfully dedicated to the citizens of Marysville, 1852. Published by Eddy Bros., stationers, Marysville, California. Lithographed by Alex. Zakreski at his Topographical Office, Washington and' Montgomery Streets (Peters, op. cit.)

[48]Charles P. Kimball, The San Francisco City Directory, San Francisco, 1850, p. 120.

[49]Henry G. Langley and Samuel A. Morison, The State Register and Year Book of Facts for the Year 1859, San Francisco 1859, p. 55.

Pendergast. In 1851, Zakrzewski lithographed a certificate of membership in the Committee of Vigilance of San Francisco.

Very probably, Zakrzewski, was also one of the first photographers in California, as he returned in that character to Poland in 1863. He died at Cracow on April 22, 1866.[50]

Michael Kraszewski

Michael (Miguel) Kraszewski, most probably a Forty-Niner, from the former Russian part of Poland, conducted a store at San Juan Capistrano in 1856 Bancroft mentions him in his *California Pastoral* as one of the victims of the Mexican band of outlaws called Manilas. In December of the above year Manilas entered Kraszewski's store and plundered it. The next day, after killing a German, they returned to Kraszewski's place and again robbed it of everything left after their first visit. Kraszewski saved his life by hiding in a clothes-basket, under a heap of soiled clothes. The band was finally caught and hanged by enraged citizens.

Bancroft, at whose request the Pole wrote a history of the gang, made use of Kraszewski's narrative as historical material; his manuscript entitled *Acts of Manilas* is preserved in the Bancroft Library at Berkeley.[51]

Paul Petrovits

Conditions of public safety and morality in California just after its deluge by hordes of immigrants were, indeed, very bad. It was but natural; the moving spirit of the masses was gold, and it evoked the worst instincts of the mob.

---

[50]Bolesław Olszewicz, **Polska Kartografia Wojskowa,** p. p. 138, 142-3; Vogdes, **The Bibliography and Cartography of California,** p. 232.

[51]H. H. Bancroft, **California Pastoral,** San Francisco, 1888, p. p. 675-77; Harris Newmark, **Sixty Years in Southern California,** p. 206.

Along with the gold seekers came many adventurers of all kinds and of both sexes; outcasts of every degree and fugitives from all parts of the globe, ready to commit any conceivable crime. There was a period in the early history of San Francisco when these criminal elements ruled the city and carried on their nefarious work with impunity. There was no civil executive power worthy of the name. But bad elements were rather an exception than the rule. The bolder and more energetic among the citizens, to the number of about two hundred, becoming impatient with this lawlessness formed a Vigilance Committee in 1851; taking law into their own hands and dealing in a dictatorial but, on the whole, just way, they cleaned up the city in a brief time. One of the most active members of the Committee was Paul Petrovits (Pietrowicz?), an official of the firm Bolton and Baron, most probably also a Forty-Niner.[52]

Jayzinsky

Still another probable Forty-Niner and a pioneer merchant of Los Angeles was Jayzinsky, the first clockmaker of the city in the fifties. His art, however, was a lost one among the people of Southern California who regulated their life only by the cock's crow or by the sun; Jayzinsky failed in his business,. but afterwards became a partner in the hardware business with N. A. Potter.[53]

Zabriskies

An important role in the history of California was played by several members of the well-

---

[52]**Academy of Pacific Coast History Publications,** Berkeley, vol. I (1910), p. 43; vol. IV (1919), p. p. 180, 181, 183, 209, 300, 523, 641.

[53]Laura Evertsen King, "The Stores of Los Angeles in 1850," **Publications of the Historical Society of Southern California,** Los Angeles, vol. V, 1900-2, p. p. 5-6. It is possible that Jayzinsky was identical with Uszynski mentioned as jeweler in San Francisco in 1863.

known Polish colonial family of Zabriskies, the most prominent of which was Colonel James C. Zabriskie, a lawyer by profession, "afterwards widely known in the state".[54] He distinguished himself by his "independence of thought and action".[55] He first came into the public eye by his bold and resolute speech at a meeting of squatters and "law and order" group in Sacramento, December 4th, 1849.[56] In 1850, he was a speaker at the Fourth of July celebration of the order of the Sons of Temperance in Sacramento.[57] His accomplished daughter, Lizzie, became the wife of Governor J. Neely Johnson. In 1856, Johnson delegated his father-in-law to deal with the Vigilance Committee in San Francisco.[58] He was accompanied in this mission by James Allen and C. B. Zabriskie, a physician and another prominent citizen of Sacramento.[59]

Other Zabriskies prominent in the early days of the state were: William F. Zabriskie, an attorney of San Francisco,[60] who was the principal speaker during the Fourth of July celebration

[54]Theodore H. Hittell, **History of California,** 1897, vol. III, p. 670.

[55]Cornelius Cole, **Memoirs,** New York, 1908, p. 127. Senator Cole calls him a "Polish refugee."

[56]Hittell, **History of California,** vol. III, p. p. 670-1; Josiah Royce, **California,** Boston and New York, 1888, p. 475.

[57]Samuel C. Upham, **Notes of a Voyage to California via Cape Horn in the Years 1849-50,** Philadelphia, 1878, p. 332.

[58]**California Historical Society Quarterly,** vol. XV, 1936, p. p. 151-2.

[59]Langley and Morison, **The State Register,** 1859, p 358; Henry J. Oglesby, "Forty Niner," **Papers in Illinois History and Transactions for the Year 1938,** The Illinois State Historical Society, Springfield, 1939, p. 170. Oglesby mentions that Dr. C. B. Zabriskie came from Jacksonville, Ill., and that he was a prominent citizen of Sacramento.

[60]Langley and Morison, **The State Register,** 1859, p. 376; Knight, **Handbook Almanac for the Pacific States,** 1863, p. 213.

at Washington, Cal., in 1850;[61] A. C. Zabriskie, a physician from New Jersey, the home state of the family, listed in the Marysville directory for 1855;[62] and A. L. Zabriskie, proprietor of the "Zabriskie Hotel", five miles northwest of Marysville.[63]

There is a small town called Zabriskie in Inyo County, near the border of Nevada.

Other Polish Forty-Niners

The extant registers of the Forty - Niners contain in addition, the following Polish or supposedly Polish names:

Captain C. W. H. Solinski (Solinskey), F. Dekut and Colonel G. Dreka, who sailed from Philadelphia January 16th, 1849, aboard the brig *Osceola*.[64] Solinski, a veteran of the Mexican War, was postmaster at Chinese Camp, Tuolomne County, in 1859.[65]

During the same month Paul Pieda sailed aboard the *Jane Parker* from Baltimore,[66] and on April 2nd, A. Skarzynski (Skarzinsk) left New Orleans by the steamer *Robert Morris*.[67]

The earliest to try to reach California by land was E. F. Lasak, who was a member of one of the mining companies from New York. He left on February 10th, 1849,[68] but evidently changed his plans later as his name appears also

---

[61]Samuel C. Upham, Notes of a Voyage to California, p. 332.

[62]California Historical Society Quarterly, vol. VIII (1929), p. 360.

[63]Ib., vol. VIII, p. 360; vol. X, 1931, p. p. 170, 362, 370; Amy's Marysville Directory for 1858, p. 92.

[64]The Argonauts of California, p. 488. George Dreka is mentioned also by Samuel C. Upham, Notes of a Voyage to California, p. 24.

[65]Langley and Morison, The State Register, 1859, p 62. Solinskey's war record is given by M. Haiman, The Poles in the Early History of Texas, Chicago, 1936, p. 48.

[66]The Argonauts of California, p. 491.

[67]Ib., p. 489.

[68]Ib., p. 423.

among the members of Havilah Mining Co., of New Orleans; this company started its march on April 20th.[69] Besides him the following came to California by land:

H. S. Brolaski, mentioned before, with a company from St. Louis who started on April 5th.[70]

A Wichrowski of New York, a member of a local German company, who departed on April 20th.[71]

J. M. Kozad of Illinois started from St. Joseph, Mo., April 16th.[72]

Among those who came by the land and sea route was a certain Count Dwarkowsky, a passenger aboard the *Von Humboldt* which left Panama during August 1849.[73]

C. A. L. Gransky, later a member of the Pioneers' Society of Sacramento, reached California by an unknown route.[74]

Anonymous pioneers

The above are all the Polish Forty-Niners— a few of them perhaps of doubtful Polish nationality — the author was able to find. Undoubtedly future researches will uncover other additional names; some Polish Forty-Niners could never be identified. So for instance, Friedrich Gerstaecker, the German traveler, tells of a Pole[75] of unknown name who came penniless to Californa together with him in 1849. In order to earn sufficient funds for a miner's equipment he worked at first as a wood chopper or digger at San Francisco. After saving the necessary money, he became a gold miner and good fortune accom-

[69] Ib., p. 402.
[70] Ib., p. 402.
[71] Ib., p. 404.
[72] Ib., p. 409.
[73] Ib., p. 494.
[74] Ib., p. 371.
[75] Gerstaecker's Travels, London, 1854, p. 256.

panied him. He often found rich veins of the precious metal. Unfortunately, however, he squandered all the fruits of his labor; for after the day's hard work, when miners filled barrooms and casinos, he wantonly spent his gold, entertaining all present with champagne. But his conduct was no exception; rather it was the rule. All gold miners were fond of a merry life and what was acquired easily, was also spent easily.

A young Pole, "who had traveled around the world and who said he was going to continue traveling until Poland was no longer lost," accompanied Carl Meyer on his trip to the Napa Valley, early in 1851.[75a]

Similarly Calixtus Wolski, a Polish soldier, civil engineer and traveler, while mentioning that he found many Poles in California and that they met with various degrees of luck writes more in detail of two Poles without giving their names or the time of their arrival to the State.[76] One was a physician who after supplementing his professional knowledge at Montpelier, settled at Lyons, France, and practiced medicine there, with great success. His earnings amounted to nearly a score of thousands of francs yearly, but nevertheless he preferred to emigrate to California. He was a homeopath and again met with such a success in his practice among the gold miners that in ten years he became the owner of more than half of the houses at Drytown, Amador County, which brought him large profits. The other was a brother of a famous Polish violinist, who emigrated to California from France, but met with so many discouraging reverses that he shortly returned to Europe, penniless, having lost much in weight, working as a cook on a ship to pay his passage.

[75a] Carl Meyer, **Nach dem Sacramento**, Aarau, 1855, p. 199.

[76] Kalixt Wolski, **Do Ameryki i w Ameryce**, p. 385.

V.
POLES WHO CAME AFTER 1849
Alexander J. J. Holinski

Of the Poles who came to California after 1849, the first to be mentioned is Alexander John Joachim Holinski (Hołyński), a traveler and friend of Julius Słowacki, the great Polish romantic poet. Born in Witebsk, in the former Polish White Ruthenia, in 1813, he took part in the November Insurrection after which he left the country. In 1836-7, together with his older brother, Stephen, and partly with Słowacki, he visited Egypt and the Holy Land; the poet dedicated to them some of his verses written during the journey. Returning to Europe, Alexander lived for a brief time in France and Spain before coming to the United States where he stayed long enough to become a citizen of the country. In 1850, he reached California by way of Panama and described the new land in a book *La Californie et les Routes Interoceaniques,* which ran through two editions in Bruxelles in 1853. Besides Wierzbicki's book, his work is another valuable Polish source on California in the Gold Rush era. The projected canal through Panama found in Holinski a staunch supporter. Holinski's stay in California was comparatively brief. He traveled also in South America and published other books. He died in Lwów, Poland, in 1884.[77]

Abandoning the chronological order, of the others who came after 1849, the most important were:

Capt. Casimir Bielawski

Besides Zakrzewski, several other Poles deserve recognition as early California cartograph-

---

[77]Orgelbranda **Encyklopedja Powszechna,** Warszawa, 1900, vol. VII, p. 135; Stanisław Zieliński, **Mały Słownik Pionierów Polskich,** p. 150.

ers.[78] Important services were rendered by Captain Casimir Bielawski. Born in Poland on February 27, 1815, he was Captain of Engineers in the

Austrian a r m y. To forestall an insurrection in t h e Austrian part of Poland in 1846, the Vienna government resorted to a vile stratagem; it instigated a r e b e l l i o n among P o l i s h peasants against the n o b l e s and landlords. M a n y p a t r i o t s were brutally b u t c h- ered, before t h e government w a s finally obliged to put down the rebellion in order to avoid a scandal- ous exposure of its machinations. The unhappy affair so disgusted Bielawski that he doffed the Austrian uniform and left the confines of the em-

CASIMIR BIELAWSKI

[78]A mention should be made of Joseph Truskolaski, deputy surveyor of the United States Land Office, who was transferred from Louisiana to California in 1852. All efforts of this author to trace him in California were of no avail. The California State Library at Sacramento, the Bancroft Library at Berkeley and Henry E. Huntington Library and Art Gallery at San Marino to whom the author appealed for help, all were unable to find any local material concerning him. Perhaps Truskolaski never reached his destination. Following are details about him which the author was able to collect and which may help some future researchers: He was a veteran of the Polish November Insurrection of 1830-1, and came to America as one of 235 Polish exiles deported by Austria to New York

pire never to return. He came to California in 1853 and for 45 years was connected with the United States Land Office at San Francisco.[79] Helena Modjeska, the famous Shakespearean actress, who knew him personally, tells in her memoirs that he was considered the most important person in the Land Office, that he personally surveyed and was generally recognized as the best authority on real property titles in the state. And, what made his knowledge and experience more valuable, she adds, was his absolute honesty; he could have easily accumulated a very large fortune, but he was deaf and blind to any attempts of graft. In 1865, Bielawski. together with J. D. Hoffman and A. Poelt, published a *Topographical and Railroad Map of the Central Part of California and Nevada.*[80]

Capt. Bielawski took a lively part in the Polish community life in early California. He was president of the Polish Society of California and

---

in 1834, for their political activities. He found a hospitable refuge in the home of James Fenimore Cooper at Cooperstown, N. Y. The famous novelist helped him to learn the English language and to shape the American career of the young exile. In time Truskolaski became a successful surveyor. It is known that about 1840, he was employed at Natchez, Miss., as City and County Surveyor, and already at that time was regarded as "not only theoretically skilled, but scrupulously accurate in practice." In 1843, he became deputy surveyor in Louisiana in employ of the United States Land Office and worked there till 1852, when he was transferred to California. (James Fenimore Cooper (the grandson), **Correspondence of James Fenimore Cooper**, New Haven 1922, vol. I, index; **Annual Reports of the Commissioner of the General Lanf Office** for the years 1843-52; Letters from Deputy Surveyors, 1844-53, Surveyor General's Office, Donaldsonville, La., Cabinet No. 116).

[79]**Annual Reports of the Commissioner of General Land Office,** for the year 1858, p. 226; for the year 1860, p. 174. In 1863, he occupied the position of principal draughtsman with $2,000 of yearly salary (**Knight, Handbook Almanac for the Pacific States,** 1863, p. 66). The earliest mention of him in the **San Francisco Directories** is in 1856.

[80]University of California, **Library Bulletin No. 9, p. 8.**

in that capacity presided over a public meeting at the Russ House, on January 22, 1864, to commemorate the first anniversary of the outbreak of the Polish January Insurrection.[81] He was also

Redrawn by Stanislaus A. Blonski

MOUNT BIELAWSKI, CAL.

one of those Poles who helped Modjeska to start her American career. He remained forever a sincere friend of the great actress and she paid him a warm tribute in her memoirs.[82] Mount Bielawski, near Los Gatos, in Santa Clara County, was named after him; it is 3,269 feet high with a fire lookout station erected on its peak.[83]

Bielawski was married to an English woman who departed this life before him dying in 1894,

[81]Rapperswyl Collections, National Library, Warsaw, Poland, MSS 424, V.

[82]Helena Modjeska, **Memories and Impressions,** p. 305-8.

[83]Mount Bielawski may be found on **Preliminary Mineralogical and Geological Map of the State of California,** by William Irelan, Jr., State Mineralogist, Jan 1, 1891.

at the age of 65 years. He himself died in San Francisco, March 3, 1905.[84]

The Kierski Brothers

In 1861, the firm of Kierski and Bro. of Stockton published a map of the city of Stockton and environs.[85] Some time in the sixties they also published *A Map of the Seat of the War in Europe*, pertaining to the Austro-Prussian War of 1866, and with an imprint of San Francisco. The owners of the firm were William and John Siegried Kierski who both came to California from New York. The oldest known reference to them as residents of Stockton may be found in the city directory for 1856, which lists them as owners of a book and stationery store at the corner Levee and Eldorado streets. The firm's name was in time reduced to "William Kierski", and the firm itself, after several changes of its location, it seems, went out of existence between 1873 and 1878. According to the Great Registers of Voters of San Joaquin County, William was 31, and John 28 years of age in 1867; the elder brother was registered as a native of Germany, and the younger, of Prussia, which, of course, most probably means German (or Prussian) Poland.[86]

---

[84]A new monument at the common grave of the Bielawskis was recently erected by the Polish Society of California of San Francisco. For Bielawski's biography see **Polski Słownik Biograficzny**, Kraków, 1936, vol. II, p. 37.

[85]University of California, **Library Bulletin No. 9**, p. 23. The full title of the Kierski brothers' map is **Map of the City of Stockton and environs, with additions and corrections to March 1861, by Duncan Beaumont. Published by Kierski and Bro.**

[86]Knight, **Handbook Almanac for the Pacific States,** 1863, p. 221; informations by letters from the Stockton Free Public Library, May 26, 1939; Henry E. Huntington Library and Art Gallery, May 17, 1939; California Historical Society, January 2, 1940, and California State Library, June 5, 1939, to the author, based on **Stockton City Directories** for the years 1856, 1870, 1871-2, 1873-4, 1876-7, 1878, 1885; **San Francisco Almanac** for the year 1859, containing a Business Directory of Stockton, p. 156; **San Francisco Directories; Great Registers of Voters of San**

Louis Alexander Sengteller

Louis Alexander Sengteller, son of a Polish exile, made many surveys and maps of California in 1868-89. He was born on April 3, 1846, in Paris, France, where his father, Alexander Seng-

LOUIS A. SENGTELLER

teller, a famous engraver of maps on steel, lived in exile after the Polish Insurrection of 1830-1. In 1856, the father was engaged in Paris for the United States Coast Survey and immediately reported for duty at the main office in Washington, D. C.[87] For twenty seven years he remained continuously in the employ of the Survey. Henry Kalussowski, a leader of the Polish immigration in America of that period, calls his "an artist"

Joaquin County for the years 1867 and 1879, etc. Besides William and John S. Kierski these documents mention: Adolph Kierski, salesman, in 1876-85; John, clerk in 1871-2 and 1878; Moritz (Morris), a merchant, all of Stockton, in 1871-2, and a capitalist, in 1874; M. Kierski and Co., stoves and tin ware, San Francisco, in 1854. Inquiries made by the author of Dr. Bolesław Olszewicz of Warsaw, an eminent Polish historian of geography, brought a reply in which the Doctor expressed the opinion that their names are purely Polish though there exists a possibility that they were germanized Poles (Dr. Olszewicz's letter to the author of July 23, 1939).

[87]Report of the Superintendent of the United States Coast and Geodetic Survey for 1884, House of Representatives Executive Documents, No. 43, 48th Congress, 2nd Session, Washington, 1885, p. 112.

of cartography and his maps most beautiful.⁸⁸
This opinion is officially supported by reports
of the Survey which say that "his work was
marked by strong characterization of topographical details, combined with harmony of tone,
and many of our best charts bear witness to his
skill."89 He died on August 11th, 1883, as an old
man of seventy years.90

Louis Alexander Sengteller followed in the
footsteps of his father. Already as a boy of six-
teen years, he assisted in the hydrographic sur-

---

⁸⁸B. Bolesławita, **Rachunki z Roku 1867**, vol. II, p. ρ.
118-9.

⁸⁹**Report of the Coast and Geodetic Survey** for 1884,
p. 16.

⁹⁰Alexander Sengteller, born at Warsaw in 1813;
studied at Biala where he was school companion of Joseph
Ignace Kraszewski, the famous novelist, and at the Liceum
of Warsaw where he became a close friend of the Mar-
grave Alexander Wielopolski, the future Russian governor
of Poland. He took part in the November Insurrection
after which he left the country. In 1831, he was at Avig-
non, France, and sacrificed half of his fortune in the
cause of helping his countrymen. He died in Washington
as an employe of the Coast Survey. He was a master of
topographical art. (Necrology in the **Kurjer Warszawski**,
Warsaw, September 11, 1883, nr. 235). The details of his
work for the United States Coast and Geodetic Survey
are given in the annual reports of the Superintendent of
the service 1856-1884 (for the most part indexed). Herbert Ogden, Chief of the Engraving Division, said of him
in his report for the year of 1884: "The Survey has lost
the services of an expert engraver in the death of Mr.
Alexander Sengteller, who died August 11, 1883. Mr.
Sengteller was engaged in Paris in 1856, and immediately
reported for duty in this office, where he remained con-
tinously employed until his death, at the age of seventy.
The many valuable charts published from the plates in-
trusted to him bear ample testimony to his artistic skill,
fully sustaining the high recommendation given him when
engaged for this special work on the survey. To within
a few months of his death he was still faithful in his
labors, and even his latest work, with old age and bodily
infirmities oppressing him, evinces that refinement of
treatment that brought him reputation in youth" (**Report**
for the year 1884, p. 112).

veys of the coast of Maine.[91] In 1863, he served in the United States Navy under Admiral Bailey in Florida, and in 1863-65, under Admiral Dahlgren in South Carolina.[92] He covered in his researches the Atlantic coast from Maine to the Mississippi delta. He also worked for some time in the Office at Washington, D. C., rising to the position of Chief of the Engraving Division (1877-78). In 1868 he was transferred to California, at first in the character of a Sub-Assistant and later as Assistant.[93] For twenty years, with a brief intermission, he rendered there "valuable service" in the field and as a cartographer.[94] His work was in reality that of a pioneer, frought with dangers and difficulties, because of the virginity of the terrain. The reports of the Survey for these years abound with descriptions of these difficulties. At times he was obliged to make his stations in trees several scores of feet high, once at the height of 103 feet.[95] In 1870, while working near Point Arena on astronomical surveys, he was forced to save his records from a burning house and again from a shipwreck.[96] In 1874, during surveys at Point Sal,

[91]Report of the Superintendent of the United States Coast Survey, for 1862, Senate Executive Documents, No. 22, 37th Congress, 3rd Session, Washington, 1864; p. 27.

[92]Military and Naval Service of the United States Coast Survey 1861-1865, Washington, 1916.

[93]San Francisco City Directory, 1868-9.

[94]Some of his maps are: Mendocino Bay, California, 1874. C. P. Patterson, Supt., U. S. Coast Survey. Triangulation, topography and hydrography by L. A. Sengteller, 1871-2; San Luis Obispo and Approaches, California, 1876. C. P. Patterson, Supt. U. S. Coast Survey. By L. A. Sengteller, 1871-5. Astronomical observations by G. Davidson 1852, 1874; and others.

[95]Reports of the Superintendent of the United States Coast Survey for the year 1873, House of Representatives Executive Documents, No. 133, 43rd Congress, 1st Session, Washington, 1875; p. 54; Report etc. for the year 1877, Senate Executive Documents, No. 12, 45th Congress, 2nd Session, Washington, 1880, pp. 55-6.

[96]Report etc. for the year 1870, House of Representatives Executive Documents, No. 112, 41-st Congress, 3rd Session, Washington, 1873, p. 44.

wishing to save his men while passing a narrow deep gulch, he met with another serious accident which disabled him for many months.[97] Nevertheless, he was thoroughly faithful to his work. Many volumes of his original notes deposited at the Office of the Survey bear testimony of his great abilities and loyalty. Besides his work in California, he also made many surveys of the Pacific coast in Oregon. The difficulties of the task undermined his health. During a hydrographic examination of Hospital Cove, Angel Island, San Francisco Bay, in 1888-9, Sengteller's health began to fail rapidly and on May 23rd, 1889, he died at the age of forty three years.

"By this event", according to an official report, "the Survey lost an officer of tried fidelity, whose capacity of a topographer was shown by the superior character of all work which he accomplished."[98] Louis Alexander Sengteller left a widow, Lucy B. Sengteller, who lived at San Francisco.[99]

Others who came after 1849

In 1850, arrived Lezinsky who became one of the pioneer merchants of San Francisco; his son George was a lawyer and introduced many beneficial reforms in the law procedure of the State.[100]

The minutes of the Democratic Society of the Polish Exiles in New York show that in 1853,

[97]Report etc. for the year 1874, House of Representatives Executive Documents, No. 100, 43rd Congress, 2nd Session, Washington, 1877, p. 37.

[98]Annual Report of the Superintendent of the Coast and Geodetic Survey for the year 1889, House of Representatives Executive Documents, No. 55, 51-st Congress, 1st Session, Washington, 1890, p. 63.

[99]San Francisco City Directory, 1890. Further details of Louis Alexander Sengteller's services with the U. S. Coast and Geodetic Survey may be found in the annual reports of the Superintendent of the Survey for the years of 1862-1889.

[100]The Bay of San Francisco, Chicago, 1892, vol. II, p. 99.

the following of its members settled in California: Bogacki, Adolph Barz, Gruenbaum and Krzeslowski.[101]

In 1854, according to a relation of Count Stanislaus R. Lanckoronski [102] of Washington, D. C., there lived, besides those already mentioned: the eccentric Doctor Teclaw from Volhynia, in Eastern Poland, at La Paz;[103] Dombrowski, owner of a coffee shop, and Uszynski, a jeweler, at San Francisco; Zagorski and John Kaczynski, gold miners, and Piotrowski, doctor of medicine, at Marysville; Henry Baranowski at Sacramento; and Zygmuntowski, doctor of medicine, and Malczewski, gold miner, in some other parts of the state. Most of these were from Russian Poland and, for the most part, veterans of Polish uprisings.

The same source mentions: Ladislaus Poplawski, who died in San Francisco in 1854; Spozarski, from Austrian Poland, and Lewicki, from

---

[101]**Księga Protokułowa Tow. Demokratycznego Wygnańców Polskich w New Yorku**, 1854, manuscript in the Library of the Polish National Alliance, Chicago.

[102]Princes Czartoryski Museum, Cracow, MSS. No. 568, p. 581.

[103]Julian Horain who visited California in 1876, wrote of him: "The locality of the town of La Paz (500 inhabitants) is said to be a real earthly paradise. For over twenty years there lives our countryman Dr. Teclaw from Volhynia who sometimes comes to San Francisco to renew friendship with his old Polish comrades. Alas, he did not show up this year and I lost an occasion to make an acquaintance with him; but I was told that he is full of praises 'for California and her inhabitants. The best proof of it is that he has saved a little fortune and though about 80 years old does not move anywhere else. I was also told that Dr. Teclaw is a little eccentric, that wishing to be killed by lightning he orders to transfer his iron bed to the garden during every storm; there he takes off his clothing and lies naked on the bed waiting for death. Lightnings spared him heretofore, but rain gives him an excellent shower which in no manner accelerates the death. It seems that the doctor is a cunning fellow and, in fact, would not like to die." (Polish Academy of Science, Cracow, MSS No. 1675, p. p. 253-60).

Prussian Poland, both of whom died in California in 1852, respectively in 1851.

At various dubious dates in the beginnings of the second half of the past century, there settled also: Szreder, a soldier of the Second Regiment of Mounted Sharpshooters in the November Insurrection, who fell a victim of an accident in the gold mines;[104] Vincent Lutnicki, a former Lieutenant of the Second Regiment of Uhlans in the same war, who still lived in 1880, and conducted a jewelry store at Sutter Creek;[105] Francis Wojciechowski, another participant of Poland's struggle for freedom in 1831, as Captain of the Sharpshooters Regiment of Sandomir; he owned a stable of pedigreed horses near San Francisco; Henry Sienkiewicz portrayed him as Longinus Podbipienta in his immortal novel *With Fire and Sword*;[106] C. Meyer and Julian W. Andrzejewski, both from former Russian Poland and also, it seems veterans of the Polish army both of whom made small fortunes as businessmen;[107] Captain Theophilus Lessen from the vicinity of Kalisz, Poland, who fought with distinction for the freedom of Hungary in 1848;[108] General Wladimir Krzyzanowski, hero of the American Civil War;[108a] Dr. Pawlicki, veteran of another Polish

[104]Hieronim Kunaszowski, Życiorysy Uczestników Powstania Listopadowego, Lwów, 1880, p. 89.

[105]Ib., p. 149.

[106]Ib., p. 151; Helena Modjeska, Memories and Impressions, p. 313.

[107]B. Bolesławita, Rachunki z r. 1867, vol. II, p. p. 120 and 126.

[108]Modjeska, Memories and Impressions, p. p. 282 and 314. Lessen was an officer in the First Regiment of Uhlans of the Polish Legion, commanded by Gen. Wysocki. He was wounded several times and fought bravely at Szolnok, Komarom, Szeged and in other battles. He was decorated with the Hungarian Military Order.

[108a] Brief biographies of Gen. W. Krzyżanowski may be found in M. Haiman's Polish Past in America, 1608-1865, Chicago, 1939, p. p. 118-23, and Historia Udziału Polaków w Amerykańskiej Wojnie Domowej, Chicago, 1928, p. p. 42-61.

Insurrection of 1863;[109] Miss Christine Narbutt, author of a novel *W Ameryce* (In America);[110] A. E. Schwatka of Greenhorn who was supervisor of Siskiyou County in 1859;[111] Jacob Lussa from Great Poland who died in the vicinity of Deer Flat on March 28, 1864, at the age of 35 years, and a certain Stanislawski of Canyon;[112] Murasky (Morawski), the father of Judge Frank J. Murasky of San Francisco;[113] Kowalsky (Kowalski), father of Col. Henry I. Kowalsky, Judge Advocate General on the staff of Governor R. W. Waterman;[114] the Bckofski brothers who conducted a general merchandise store at Upper Lake, Lake County, and the Levinsky brothers, also owners of a general merchandise store at Woodbridge, San Joaquin County, in 1863;[115] and many others all traces of whom became lost.

Nearly all of the above mentioned were Polish political exiles, mostly of noble origin, men of education and, often formerly of means and high social position. Besides these, Polish economic immigrants, artisans and small businessmen, reached California soon after the Gold Rush. A typical example of this class was Michael Przybylowicz; born in Poznan, Poland, in 1826, he landed at New York in 1851 and in 1853 appeared in California where for three years he conducted a meat-market and a restaurant at San Francisco and Stockton. Later he returned to the East and became a pioneer and a prominent citizen of

---

[109]Modjeska, **Memories and Impressions**, p. p. 282, 307 and 313-4.

[110]Published at Warsaw in 1875.

[111]Langley and Morison, **The State Register**, 1859, p. 393.

[112]Rapperswyl Collections, National Library, Warsaw, MSS No. 424, V (Letter of J. W. Andrzejewski to the editor of the **Echö z Polski**, April, 1864).

[113]**The Bay of San Francisco**, vol. I, p. 585.

[114]Ib., vol. II, p. 302.

[115]Knight, **Handbook Almanac for the Pacific States**, 1863, p. p. 164 and 222.

Leavenworth, Kas. He built the first brick building there and held several public offices in the city and state.116 Another California pioneer of this class was Francis Czerwinski (1825-1909), native of Great Poland, who reached the state by Cuba and Panama about 1853, and remained there for five years, earning some money He later lived and died at Milwaukee, Wis.117

An early Polish contribution to the artistic life of California was Madame Korsinski, "a charming vocalist", who sang at the opening of the Jenny Lind Theatre at San Francisco on October 28th, 1850.118 In 1851, she gave a successful concert at Marysville and "delighted a large audience by her manner of singing selections from operas, accompanied on the piano by her husband."119

The California Gold-Rush became the spark which released the great influx of the Polish peasant, or economic immigration to this country, though the movement began to materialize several years later and was directed rather to the Eastern and Middle States, than to the extreme West. It also found other echoes among the Poles. Already in 1850, Casimir Tomkiewicz, Leonard Niedzwiecki and other Polish exiles in Paris formed a plan to found a Polish colony in California under the protectorate of Prince Adam George Czartoryski.119a Farming was to be the main purpose of the colony, the authors of the plan hoped, however, that gold might help them to realize the undertaking. Other early Polish plans of colonizing California are known.

116Andreas, **History of Kansas**, 1883, p. 452; Chapman, **Portrait and Biographical Record of Leavenworth, Douglas and Franklin Counties, Kansas**, 1899, p. 526.
117Ks. Wacław Kruszka, **Historia Polska w Ameryce**, wyd. drugie, Milwaukee, 1937, vol. I, p. 379.
118Bancroft, **History of California**, vol. VI, p. 245.
119California Historical Society Quarterly, vol. XV, p. 46.
119aThe Princes Czartoryski Museum, Cracow, MMS No. 5660.

VI.
CALIFORNIA POLES IN THE CIVIL WAR

It is impossible to glean all the Polish names from the rolls of California regiments serving in the Civil War. The main difficulties one encounters in this task are careless spelling of the names, foreign names borne by many Poles and the neglect to give the country of origin with each name in the records.

Only typical and indubitable Polish names are given in the list below:

Baranowski, Henry, Private, Co. C, Third Regiment of Infantry, enlisted at Camp Halleck, Cal., June 15, 1862; reenlisted as Veteran Volunteer, Co. A, at Camp Douglas, Utah Territory, August 1, 1864; deserted at Salt Lake City, Utah Territory, January 1, 1866.[120]

Beinkoskey (Bieńkowski), Alexander, Private, Co. G, Third Regiment of Infantry, enlisted at San Francisco, May 29, 1862; deserted at Camp Halleck, Cal., June 15, 1862.[121]

Derproskey (Dabrowski?), William F., Private, Co. I, Second Regiment of Cavalry, enlisted at Placerville, Cal., September 15, 1861, mustered out at San Francisco, October 7, 1864.[122]

Holski, Edward, Private, Co. B, Third Regiment of Infantry, enlisted at Sacramento, October 4, 1862, discharged at Camp Union, December 19. 1862, for disability.[123]

Klima, Michael, Private Co. A, Seventh Regiment of Infantry, enlisted at Sacramento, October 20, 1864, discharged at San Francisco, April 13, 1866.[124]

---

[120]R. H. Orton, **Records of California Men in the War of Rebellion,** Sacramento, 1890, p. p. 526 and 545.
[121]Ib., p. 576.
[122]Ib., p. 270.
[123]Ib., p. 538.
[124]Ib., p. 768.

Kustel, Cassimer B., Private, Co. D., Eighth Regiment of Infantry, enlisted at San Francisco, December 1, 1864, discharged at San Francisco, October 24, 1865.[125]

Liberski, Robert, Private, Co. I, Eighth Regiment of Infantry, enlisted at Marysville, Cal., December 30, 1864, discharged at San Francisco, October 24, 1865.[126]

Macowitzki (Makowiecki), Charles, Corporal, Co. K, First Regiment of Cavalry, enlisted at San Francisco, July 24, 1863, mustered out at Santa Fe, New Mexico, July 25, 1866.[127]

Marcovitch (Markowicz), John, Private, Co. A, First Regiment of Cavalry, enlisted at Oroville, Cal., February 13, 1865, mustered out at San Francisco, May 22, 1866.[128]

Omazta (Omasta), Joseph, Private, Co. C, Third Regiment of Infantry, enlisted at San Francisco, June 1, 1862, mustered out at Camp Douglas, Utah Territory, May 31, 1865.[129]

Philliporski (Filipowski), Lyon (Leon), Private, Co. A, Fifth Regiment of Infantry, enlisted at Yreka, Cal., October 20, 1861, discharged at Mesilla, N. M., November 30, 1864.[130]

Rozmoski (Rozumowski?), Kasmier, Private, Co. G, Fourth Regiment of Infantry, enlisted at Drum Barracks, Cal., February 23, 1864, discharged at San Francisco, March 31, 1866.[131]

Sabowleski (Sobolewski), Paul F. H., Private, Co. E, Sixth Regiment of Infantry, enlisted at San Francisco, April 7, 1863, discharged at San Francisco, October 31, 1865.[132]

Zabriskie, James A., First Lieutenant and Staff Adjutant, Fifth Regiment of Infantry, en-

---

[125]Ib., p. 809.
[126]Ib., p. 822.
[127]Ib., p. 152.
[128]Ib., p. 94.
[129]Ib., p. p. 550 and 569.
[130]Ib., p. 681.
[131]Ib., p. 649.
[132]Ib., p. 745.

listed at Sacramento, September 12, 1861, mustered out at Franklin, Tex., December 14, 1864.[133]

Following are some doubtful names:

Biastock, Charles, Private, Co. H, Fifth Regiment of Infantry, enlisted at Virginia City, Nevada, October 1861, discharged at Franklin, Tex., December 12, 1864.[134]

Drahor, Adam J., Sergeant, Company F, Second Regiment of Cavalry, enlisted at Washington, Cal., August 1, 1863, discharged at Sacramento, December 9, 1864. for disability.[135]

Duskey, Robert F., Sergeant, Co. C, Third Regiment of Infantry, enlisted at Sacramento, September 30, 1862, reduced to the ranks at his own request and transferred to Co. A at Camp Douglas, Utah Territory, June 3, 1865, mustered out at Denver, Colo., October 7, 1865.[136]

Leya, Frantz, Private, Co. M, Second Regiment of Cavalry, enlisted at San Francisco, April 25, 1862, mustered out at Camp Douglas, Utah Territory, May 29, 1865.[137]

Luskey, George, Private, Co. D, Fifth Regiment of Infantry, enlisted at Sacramento, September 19, 1861, reenlisted as Veteran Volunteer, at Tucson, Arizona Territory, February 28, 1864, and transferred to Co. D, First Battalion of Veteran Infantry, discharged at Los Pinos, N. M., September 15, 1866.[138]

Rosetzky, Charles H., Private, Co. I, Third Regiment of Infantry, enlisted at San Francisco, October 10, 1862, mustered out at Camp Douglas, Utah Territory, October 18, 1864; reenlisted as Private, Co. B, Eighth Regiment of Infantry, at Sacramento, November 15, 1864, deserted at

[133]Ib., p. 676; also Knight, **Handbook Almanac for the Pacific States**, 1863, p. 61.
[134]Ib., p. 710.
[135]Ib., p. 243.
[136]Ib., p. p. 528, 543 and 554.
[137]Ib., p. 299.
[138]Ib., p. p. 401 and 692.

Fort Point, San Francisco, March 30, 1865.[139]

Tuskey, John, Private, Co. I, Second Regiment of Cavalry, enlisted at Placerville, Cal., September 15, 1861, deserted at Camp Latham, Cal., May 3, 1862.[140]

Zorkowsky, Nathan, Sergeant, Co. B, First Regiment of Cavalry, enlisted at San Francisco, September 5, 1861, mustered out at San Francisco, December 31, 1866.[141]

---

[139]Ib., p. p. 588 and 804.
[140]Ib., p. 274.
[141]Ib., p. 98.

VII.

CALIFORNIA POLES AND THE JANUARY INSURRECTION

In 1863, a new uprising against the Russian rule broke out in Poland; it is known in history as the January Insurrection from the month of its outbreak. It was but natural that the movement found its echo among the American Poles. Some of them tried to reach Poland in order to offer their services to the cause of liberty. Committees were organized in some cities to collect funds for the succor of the insurgent armies. A Polish Committee functioned also at San Francisco. Its most active members were: Rudolph Korwin Piotrowski, C. Meyer, J. W. Andrzejowski, Secretary of the Committee; Dr. J. L. Czapkay, a Hungarian exile, and Capt. Casimir Bielawski. Meyer later was nominated an official representative for California of the Polish National Government which secretly led the uprising. The San Francisco Committee became the nucleus of the still existing Polish Society of California.[142]

---

[142]MSS of the Rapperswyl Collections, National Library, Warsaw, No. 424, V, contain a "List of donations of members of the Polish Society and friends at San Francisco for the purpose of direct support of the Polish cause for March, 1864," which is probably an almost complete roster of the members of the society. It is as follows (the list gives what part of Poland the member came from and his place of abode):

Andrzejowski Julian W. — Kingdom of Poland — San Francisco.

Bielawski Casimir — Galicia — San Francisco.

Bojarski Ladislaus—Kingdom of Poland—San Francisco.

Betkowski Peter — Gr. Duchy of Poznan — San Francisco.

Czaykowski Leon—Kingdom of Poland—San Francisco.

Czaykowski Vincent — Gr. Duchy of Poznan — San Francisco.

Another Polish Committee was formed at Sacramento under the presidency of the eloquent and erudite Senator Newton Booth.

The action of these Committees met with sincere support of the Californians. They were able to collect about $8,000,143 for the Polish cause during the Insurrection, which amounted to nearly half of the sum collected in the whole country. The Civil War then raging in this country and the quick suppression of the movement in Poland by overwhelmingly superior Russian forces prevented the American Poles from collecting a larger sum.

It was under the leadership of the San Francisco Committee that the first Polish celebration in California was organized at that city on January 22nd, 1864, to commemorate the first anni-

---

Cohn, Dr. M. — Kingdom of Poland — San Francisco.

Dobrzynski Gust.—Kingdom of Poland — San Francisco.

Eisenberg — Galicia — San Francisco.

Freedberg M. — Gr. Duchy of Poznan—San Francisco.

Friedlander — Gr. Duchy of Poznan— San Francisco.

Fox H. B. — Kingdom of Poland — San Francisco.

Gerbic Charles — Galicia — San Francisco.

Greenberg M. — Kingdom of Poland— San Francisco.

Hafter Ch. B. — Gr. Duchy of Poznan — San Francisco.

Kruszewski Anthony — Kingdom of Poland — San Francisco.

Kutner Adolph—Kingdom of Poland—San Francisco.

Kiczman Joseph — Galicia — San Francisco.

Lipmann Joseph — Galicia — San Francisco.

Luniewski Ernst L. — Kingdom of Poland — San Francisco.

Louis Moses — Kingdom of Poland — San Francisco.

Levy M. B. — Kingdom of Poland — San Francisco.

Levy Alexander — Kingdom of Poland — San Francisco.

Lewinson S., — Kingdom of Poland — San Francisco.

Liberski N. P. — Gr. Duchy of Poznan — Marsylle (Marysville?)

Meyer C. — Kingdom of Poland — San Francisco.

Mesz M. — Kingdom of Poland — San Francisco.

Mendlewicz Louis — Kingdom of Poland — San Francisco.

versary of the outbreak of the Insurrection. According to a contemporary correspondence of Andrzejowski to the *Echo z Polski* of New York,[144] the celebration was inaugurated by a band parade through the streets of the city, beginning at 1 A. M., the exact hour of the outbreak. The next morning at ten a High Mass was sung in the Roman Catholic Cathedral of St. Mary for the repose of souls of Poles killed in the Insurrection. In the evening a public dinner was given at the headquarters of the Committee at Russ Hotel with about two hundred people present. Capt. Bielawski acted as toastmaster and the speakers were: Capt. Piotrowski, Senator Booth, Col. James C. Zabriskie and Messrs. Lazard, Choinski, M. Schloss and Uszynski. Remarks

---

Mendlewicz Nickolas — Kingdom of Poland — San Francisco.

Mayer — Kingdom of Poland — San Francisco.

Marks — Kingdom of Poland — San Francisco.

Michelsen M. — Gr. Duchy of Poznan — San Francisco.

Neumann Joseph — Kingdom of Poland — San Francisco.

Neumann Salomon — Kingdom of Poland — San Francisco.

Piotrowski Rudolph K. — Kingdom of Poland — San Francisco.

Prag Marten — Kingdom of Poland — San Francisco.

Pałecki Joseph — Gr. Duchy of Poznan — San Francisco.

Pinczowski — Kingdom of Poland — San Francisco.

Philips A. — Kingdom of Poland — San Francisco.

Rottenberg Abraham — Kingdom of Poland — San Francisco.

Rosenthal Joseph — Kingdom of Poland — San Francisco.

Strentzel John Dr. — Kingdom of Poland — Martinez.

Strentzel Henry — Kingdom of Poland — Martinez.

Siukwitz Ladislaus — Kingdom of Poland — San Francisco.

Schloss M. — Kingdom of Poland — San Francisco.

Schoenberg — Kingdom of Poland — San Francisco.

Usicki John — Kingdom of Poland — San Francisco.

Wolfson Joseph—Kingdom of Poland—San Francisco.

Weintraub — Kingdom of Poland — San Francisco.

Zawadzki — Gr. Duchy of Poznan — San Francisco.

were also made by representatives of various national groups, namely by Doctor Czapkay for the Hungarians, Doctor Lehr for the Germans, Mr. Memi in behalf of the Irish and Mr. Villamori in the name of the Italians, all of whom expressed their own and their countrymen's sympathies for the Polish cause. The evening was closed by a recital of patriotic poems written especially for the occasion by various ladies, by Senator Booth. On the next morning, January 23rd, special services commemorating the occasion were held in the Jewish synagogue under leadership of the Rev. Dr. Henry.[145]

On the whole, Polish community life in San Francisco and in some other California cities, was at that time rather intimate, at least among the political exiles who felt themselves bound by common memories, ideals and sorrows. The feeling of distance separating them from other centers of Polish life in America and of the seemingly endless spaces dividing them from their old country, of itself encouraged such a mode of life. Outside of cities this contact was difficult and Putrament from Mariposa, the hero of one of Sienkiewicz's masterful short stories, was not a legend, but a realistic representative of those Poles whose lives and even names became lost on the pioneer march through the American West.

Though perhaps a small group when compared with other national contingents which left their record in the annals of California, the Poles were nevertheless a highly constructive element in the early life of the State. Modjeska says of them, that were it not for the Pacific Ocean, which closed the shores of America, they would still

---

143B. Bolesławita, **Rachunki z Roku 1867**, vol. II, p 127.

144The first newspaper in the Polish language in this country.

145Rapperswyl Collections, National Library, Warsaw, No. 424, V.

go further west in order to be as far as possible from the home of slavery into which their country was changed by oppressors. But here in the sunny land they found freedom and new homes, they found friends and a measure of prosperity. They repaid the young commonwealth with the best that was in them.

THE END.

BIBLIOGRAPHY

Academy of Pacific Coast History Publications, Berkeley, vol. I, (1910), IV (1919).

S. Austin Allibone, A Critical Dictionary of English Literature and British and American Authors, London. 1897, vol. III.

Amy's Marysville Directory for 1858.

William Frederick Bade, The Life and Letters of John Muir, Boston and New York, 1924, 2 vols.

The American Whig Review, New York, vols. III and IV (1846).

Alfred Theodore Andreas, History of the State of Kansas, Chicago, 1883.

Hubert H. Bancroft, California Pastoral, San Francisco, 1888.

Hubert H. Bancroft, History of Alaska, San Francisco, 1890.

Hubert H. Bancroft, History of California, San Francisco, 1884-90, 7 vols.

The Bay of San Francisco, Chicago, 1892, vol. II.

Leslie Edgar Bliss, Librarian, Henry E. Huntington Library and Art Gallery, San Marino, Cal., letter to the author of October 25, 1939.

Stanislaus A. Blonski, San Francisco, letters to the author of July 28, August 22, September 26 and October 6, 1938, and April 22, 1939.

B. Boleslawita, Rachunki z Roku 1867, Poznań, vol. II.

California Historical Society, San Francisco, letter to the author, January 2, 1940.

California Historical Society Quarterly, San Francisco, vols. IV, VIII, XII, XIII, XIV, XV.

California State Journal of Medicine, San Francisco, vol. I, (1856).

Chapman, Portrait and Biographical Record of Leavenworth, Douglas and Franklin Counties, Kansas, 1899.

Robert G. Cleland, A History of California, The American Period, New York, 1912.

H. W. S. Cleveland, Voyages of a Merchant Navigator of the Days that are past, compiled from the Journals and Letters of the Late Richard Jeffry Cleveland, New York, 1886.

Richard Jeffry Cleveland, A Narrative of Voyages and Commercial Enterprizes, Cambridge, 1843.

Cornelius Cole, Memoirs, New York, 1908.

Commissioners to Enquire on the City Property, Report on the Condition of the Real Estate within the Limits of the City of San Francisco, San Francisco, 1851.

James Fenimore Cooper, Correspondence of James Fenimore Cooper, New Haven, 1922, vol. I.

Lauren E. Crane, ed., **Newton Booth of California, His Speeches and Addresses**, New York and London, 1894.

William Heath Davis, **Seventy-Five Years in California**, San Francisco, 1929.

Commissioner of the General Land Office, **Annual Reports** for the years 1843-52, 1858, 1860, Washington, D. C.

Friedrich W. C. Gerstaecker, **Travels**, London, 1854.

Agaton Giller, **Album Muzeum Narodowego w Rapperswylu, Wieniec Pamiątkowy**, Rapperswyl, 1881.

Mabel R. Gillis, State Librarian, California State Library, Sacramento, letters to the author of June 5 and October 23, 1939.

J. A. Graves, **My Seventy Years in California, 1857-1927**, Los Angeles, 1927.

Mieczysław Haiman, **Feliks Paweł Wierzbicki i jego "California"**, Chicago, 1933.

Mieczysław Haiman, **Historia Udziału Polaków w Amerykanskiej Wojnie Domowej**, Chicago, 1928.

Miecislaus Haiman, **The Poles in the Early History Of Texas**, Annals of the P. R. C. U. Archives and Museum, vol. I, Chicago, 1936.

Miecislaus Haiman, **Polish Past in America, 1608-1865**, Chicago, 1939.

Theodore H. Hittell, **History of California**, San Francisco, 1885-1897, 4 vols.

Alexandre Holinski, **La California et les Routes Interoceaniques**, Bruxelles, 1853.

William Irelan, Jr., **Preliminary Mineralogical and Geological Map of the State of California**, 1891.

Laura Evertsen King, "The Stores of Los Angeles in 1850," **Publications of Historical Society of Southern California**, Los Angeles, vol. V.

William H. Knight, **Handbook Almanac for the Pacific States, 1863**, San Francisco, 1863.

Ks. Wacław Kruszka, **Historia Polska w Ameryce**, wydanie drugie, Milwaukee, 1937, vol. I.

Hieronim Kunaszowski, **Życiorysy Uczestników Powstania Listopadowego**, Lwów, 1880.

Kuryer Warszawski, Warsaw, 1883, Nos. 126 and 235.

Henry G. Langley and Samuel A. Morison, **The State Register and Year Book of Facts for the Year 1859**, San Francisco, 1859.

George D. Lyman, M. D., "Wierzbicki, The Book and the Doctor," introduction to F. P. Wierzbicki's **California as it is**, San Francisco, 1933, (The Grabhorn Press).

The Magazine of History, Tarrytown, vol. XXXII, No. 2.

Ernest de Massey, "A Frenchman in the Gold Rush," **California Historical Society Publications**, San Francisco, 1927.

Carl Meyer, **Nach dem Sacramento, Reisebilder eines Heimgekehrten**, Aarau, 1855; the same in the English translation: **Bound for Sacramento, Travel-Pictures** of a returned Wanderer, transl. from the German by Ruth Frey Oxe, Claremont, Cal., 1938.

Jan Mitkiewicz, "Kilka Słów o Kalifornii," **Biblioteka Warszawska**, Warsaw, vol. II, 1849.

Jan Mitkiewicz, "O Złocie," **Biblioteka Warszawska**, Warsaw, vol. II, 1849.

Helena Modjeska, **Memories and Impressions**, New York, 1910.

Rapperswyl Collections, National Library, Warsaw, MMS No. 424, V.

Harris Newmark, **Sixty Years in Southern California, 1853-1913**, New York, 1916.

Henry J. Oglesby, "Forty Niner", **Papers in Illinois History and Transactions for the Year 1938**, The Illinois State Historical Society, Springfield, 1939.

Bolesław Olszewicz, **Polska Kartografia Wojskowa**, Warszawa, 1921.

Dr. Bolesław Olszewicz. Librarian, Joseph Piłsudski University, Warsaw, Poland, letters to the author of July 7 and 23, 1939.

Orgelbranda **Encyklopedja Powszechna**, Warszawa, 1900, vol. VII.

R. H. Orton, **Records of California Men in the War of Rebellion**, Sacramento, 1890.

Fred S. Perrine, Secretary, Oregon City Chamber of Commerce, letter to the author of August 8, 1930.

Harry T. Peters, **California on Stone**, New York, 1935.

A Pioneer, **Argonauts of California**, New York, 1890.

Polish Academy of Sciences, Cracow, MSS No. 1675.

Polski Słowik Biograficzny, Polska Akademia Umiejętności, Kraków, 1936, vol. II.

Herbert Ingram Priestley, Librarian, The Bancroft Library, Berkeley, letters to the author of August 27 and October 3, 1930, and of May 26, July 5 and October 21, 1939.

The Princes Czartoryski Museum, Cracow, MSS Nos. 568 and 5660.

Josiah Royce, **California**, Boston and New York, 1888.

The Russians in California, California Historical Society, San Francisco, 1933.

San Francisco Directories, 1850, 1854, 1856, 1858-65, 1870, 1878, 1885, 1888, 1890.

William Shaler, "Journal of a Voyage from China to the Southwestern Coast of America made in 1804", **American Register**, Philadelphia, vol. II, 1808.

Frank Soule, John H. Gilson and James Nisbet, **The Annals of San Francisco**, New York, 1855.

Stockton City Directories, 1856, 1870-4, 1876-8, 1885.

Surveyor General's Office, Donaldsonville, La., Letters from Deputy Surveyors, 1844-53, Cabinet No. 116.

W. F. Swasey, **The Early Days and Men of California**, Oakland, 1891.

Ks. A. Syski, **Zakład sw. Kazimierza w Paryzu**, Warszawa, Łuck, 1936.
Towarzystwo Demokratyczne Wygnańców Polskich w New Yorku, **Księga Protokułowa**, 1854, MSS in the Library of the Polish National Alliance, Chicago.
Towarzystwo Historyczno - Literackie w Paryżu, **Rocznik**, Paris, 1867.
Office of the Director, U. S. Coast and Geodetic Survey, Washingtcn, D. C., letters to the author of May 24 and June 9, 1939.
Superintendent of the U. S. Coast and Geodetic Survey, **Annual Reports** for the years 1856-1890.
Military and Naval Service of the United States Coast Survey, 1861-1865, Washington, 1916.
University of California, Library Bulletin No. 9, **List of Printed Maps of California**, Berkeley, 1887.
Samuel C. Upham, **Notes of a Voyage to California via Cape Horn in The Years 1849-50**, Philadelphia, 1878.
Paul E. Vandor, **History of Fresno County, Cal.**, Los Angeles, 1919.
Anthcny W. Vogdes, **A Bibliography Relating to the Geology, Palentology, and Mineral Resources of California**. Bulletin No. 30 of the California State Mining Bureau, Sacramento, 1904.
Henry Ramp Wagner, **California Imprints, August 1846—June 1851**, Berkeley, 1922.
Henry Ramp Wagner, "The Life of Ferdinand C. Ewer", **California Historical Society Quarterly**, vols. XIII (1934) and XIV (1935).
Willard O. Waters, Bibliographer for Americana, Henry E. Huntington Library and Art Gallery, San Marino, Cal., letter to the author of May 17, 1939.
Felix Paul Wierzbicki, M. D., "Essay on History of Medicine", **California State Journal of Medicine**, San Francisco, vol. I, 1856.
Mrs. M. Burton Williamson, "History of Santa Catalina Island", **Publications of the Historical Society of Southern California**, Los Angeles, vol. VI, 1903-5.
Lcis K. Witherow, Reference Librarian, Stockton Free Public Library, letter to the author of May 26, 1939.
Kalixt Wolski, **Do Ameryki i w Ameryce**, Lwow, 1877.
Stanisław Zieliński, **Mały Słownik Pionierów Polskich**, Warszawa, 1932.

Publications of the P. R. C. U. Archives and Museum

984 MILWAUKEE AVE., CHICAGO, ILL.

Annals

Vol. I, POLES IN THE EARLY HISTORY OF TEXAS, by Miecislaus Haiman, 1936 (out of print).

Vol. II, POLISH PIONEERS OF VIRGINIA AND KENTUCKY, by Miecislaus Haiman, 1937 (out of print).

Vol. III, POLES IN NEW YORK IN THE 17th and 18th CENTURIES, by Miecislaus Haiman, 1938.

Vol. IV, A NEW ENGLAND CITY AND THE NOVEMBER UPRISING, by Arthur Prudden Coleman, 1939.

Vol. V, POLISH PIONEERS OF CALIFORNIA, by Miecislaus Haiman, 1940.

Each volume 50 cts., cloth 75 cts., postpaid.

Books

THE FALL OF POLAND IN CONTEMPO-RARY AMERICAN OPINION, by Miecislaus Haiman, 1939, p. p. XVI, 271, $1.75 (paper covers), postpaid.

POLISH PAST IN AMERICA, 1608-1865, by Miecislaus Haiman, 1939, p. p. XVI, 178, with 66 illustrations and 2 maps, $2.00 (cloth), postpaid.